PRAYING FOR
Revival

Brian H. Edwards

ISBN 978-1-84625-647-9

British Library Cataloguing in Publication Data available

Published by Day One Publications
Ryelands Road, Leominster, HR6 8NZ
Telephone 01568 613 740
Toll Free 888 329 6630 (North Americal)
email—sales@dayone.co.uk
web site—www.dayone.co.uk

Cover design by Kathryn Chedgzoy

Printed by 4edge Limited

This is a companion volume with
Revival — a people saturated with God

*This book is dedicated to a generation of young preachers
and pastors who may know little of the story of revival but
who long for the presence of God in their ministry*

Revival is a sovereign work of God's Holy Spirit resulting in an unusual awakening of spiritual life among God's people. This results in an awesome awareness of God, a deep conviction of sin, a longing for holiness, a renewed joy and love for the Father and the Son, and a passion to reach the lost. It is generally accompanied by a significant number of the lost coming to a true faith in Christ.

Contents

Introduction

This is the second of two books that work together on the subject of revival in the Christian church. They are companion volumes because whilst the first book provides a biblical framework to explore the hallmarks of historic revivals, this book adds the biblical mortar that ensures the framework holds together.

Revival—a people saturated with God, was first published in 1990 and after seven impressions was out of print for a few years. It is now fully revised and updated. It is a study of revival set in the context of the events of the reign of Hezekiah, king of Judah seven hundred years before Pentecost. It answers the question: Were there common elements between what happened in the time of Hezekiah and what has been called 'revival' in the history of the Christian church? We can hardly tell a generation about things 'our fathers have told us' so that 'the next generation would know them' (Psalm 78:3–6), unless we first read what our fathers have told us. The first book, *Revival—a people saturated with God*, is therefore descriptive because it traces the events during the reign of Hezekiah and looks for the same elements throughout the history of revival in the Christian church.

Another question has to be answered: Even if we find shared elements between a biblical revival and revivals in the history of the church, is revival necessarily a biblical experience that we can claim—and expect—at any time since Pentecost? Narratives from Bible history are instructive, but not prescriptive—they do not necessarily tell us what we should do or expect. This book is a revision of *Can we pray for Revival?* first published in 2001. It sets out to provide the evidence for revival throughout the Bible. It is a biblical theology of revival.

However, *Praying for Revival* is much more than that. The purpose is to stimulate a cry for revival set in a thorough biblical foundation. Prayer is encouraged by the introduction of a series of short cameos from those who were involved in historic revivals under the heading: 'I was there'.

If these two volumes lead to a 'concert of prayer' among church leaders and their members, the purpose will have been more than fulfilled.

'Union in prayer for the sake of a world lying in wickedness should become the watchword of the entire church of God' [1]

Brian Edwards
July 2019

---

1   Prime, *The Power of Prayer* (The Banner of Truth Trust, 1991. First published 1859), p. 196. On 'union in prayer' see also later in this book, p. 186.

1. What is revival?

No single definition of revival will quite do. To *describe* a particular revival is easy, but to *define* revival is almost impossible. In a wise caution against over-exact definitions, Iain Murray suggests that, 'If we could understand revivals, they would not be the astonishing things which they are.'[2] Similarly, Jim Packer warns that because of the different cultures in which the church finds itself in different ages, and the various ways in which it has lost its vitality: 'It is not safe for us to assume that the outward forms and phenomena of revival in this or any future age will always prove to have exact historical precedents.'[3] In other words, revivals do not all conform to a set pattern.

> Revival is an act of God's absolute sovereignty ... his Spirit is as free as the wind to blow wherever, whenever and however he pleases.

Far from this being a discouraging start, it is in fact the glory of revival. Revival is an act of God's absolute sovereignty, and because he has nowhere in the Bible provided us with a simple definition of the experience, his Spirit is as free as the wind to blow wherever, whenever and however he pleases.

Whenever we approach this subject we should do so with a sense of awe and wonder. The work of God in revival, as is true of every work of his, is always greater than our finite minds can grasp. There is always a mystery in what he does. We must be on our guard that we do not box God in more than the limits that he has set for himself in his word.

---

2   Iain H. Murray, *Pentecost—Today?* (Banner of Truth, 1998), p. 5.
3   James I. Packer, *God in our Midst* (Authentic Publishing, 1987), pp. 10–11.

What revival is not

To clear the ground, it may be helpful briefly to glance at some activities and experiences in the church that should never be confused with revival.

REVIVAL IS NOT TO BE CONFUSED WITH PHENOMENA OR EXCITEMENT

Sometimes, revivals have been accompanied by strange and unexplained events. There is a chapter in the previous book entitled 'Error, excess and the unusual' where these are discussed. Sadly, strange and noisy phenomena have too frequently stirred confusion into the quiet waters of a longing and expectation for God. They are sometimes offered as sure evidence of revival—they are not. The Azusa Street revival of 1906 in America was really a revival of tongues-speaking, and this was exported across the world.

REVIVAL IS NOT TO BE CONFUSED WITH RESTORATION OR RENEWAL

For some, revival is the restoration of certain spiritual gifts to the life of the church. It has occasionally been assumed that revival must be charismatic, baptistic and nondenominational. That is an interesting suggestion when we consider that the last major revival that took place in the United Kingdom, under the ministry of Duncan Campbell during the 1940s and 1950s in the Western Islands of Scotland, was non-charismatic, paedo-baptist and within the Church of Scotland. Before that, the last major revival in England was in East Anglia in 1921; this was non-charismatic and denominational—it began in a Baptist church.

The evangelical world is full of experiences today. They are not all bad, but even the experience that leads the Christian to a deeper awareness of the reality of Christ is not in itself revival. A renewal of spiritual life for a believer or for a church ought not to be unfamiliar in the experience of Christians—but this is not revival. The word 'renewal' has been used today to cover so many experiences that it is no longer serviceable as a synonym for revival. Richard Lovelace used the word renewal to refer to revival[4] and Jim Packer followed him[5]. Erroll Hulse helpfully reminded us that an older word to describe this kind of thing is a 'visitation'. He pleads for a careful use of terminology, but he is too restrictive in suggesting that 'Strictly speaking, it is better to describe a local revival as a visitation.'[6] How local is 'local'? It is unhelpful to define revivals either by geography or duration.

REVIVAL IS NOT TO BE CONFUSED WITH REFORMATION

Reformation is a re-forming of the doctrine or structure of the church to the theology of the New Testament. It is true that reformation has often been accompanied by revival; this was certainly the case during the time of the Reformation across Europe in the fifteenth and sixteenth centuries. Revival may lead to reformation; this happened to a degree following the eighteenth-century revival in England. But whereas reformation is primarily to do with doctrine—what we believe, revival is primarily to do with life—how we live and respond to God. Arguably, one of the clearest examples of this in the Bible is found in the difference between what happened during the reigns of Hezekiah and Josiah. Hezekiah, who was without doubt a leader, experienced revival because it was essentially a movement among the people. Under Josiah, on the other hand, changes were imposed from the top.

REVIVAL IS NOT TO BE CONFUSED WITH CHURCH GROWTH

The fact that a congregation increases from fifteen to five hundred in five years is not in itself evidence of revival. Much of that growth may be sheep-stealing. Whilst it is true that revival always results in numerical growth, there are far more important factors that indicate whether or not the work can be described as revival.

---

4   Richard Lovelace, *Dynamics of Spiritual Life* (IVP USA, 1979).
5   J. I. Packer, *God in our Midst—Seeking and Receiving Ongoing Revival* (Word Publishing, 1987).
6   Erroll Hulse, *Give Him No Rest* (Evangelical Press, 1991), pp. 18–20.

Sadly, some of our contemporary church growth 'successes' have masked the real need for spiritual revival. Our numbers, programmes, budgets and buildings are all seen as evidence that we are doing well and that little more is required. In the bookstore of one of the largest evangelical churches in America that has been a model for church growth, this writer looked in vain for books on the subject of revival.

In the wisdom of God, we have no idea of the numerical size of the churches in Revelation 2–3, but we are left in no doubt about the spiritual condition of each of them. That is significant.

REVIVAL IS NOT TO BE CONFUSED WITH MISSION

A mission, either for the deepening of the spiritual life of the church members or for the salvation of the lost, is not revival. It is a sad mistake to use the word revival to describe a mission. A church can organise a mission. But we cannot organise a revival. This is a vital distinction.

Can we create a revival?

During the 1830s, the American evangelist Charles Grandison Finney modelled what has become widely accepted as the definition of revival in North America. Whilst he undoubtedly saw many thousands converted to Christ through his preaching, Finney gradually turned the means that he employed in his meetings into a methodology for all to copy; this was particularly true of the 'altar call' which pressed for an immediate and open response to the preaching. Finney gave a series of lectures in 1834 and they were published the following year. Their danger lay in the fact that they were persuasively attractive yet theologically flawed.

Finney's analysis of the state of much of the professing church was at times very incisive, and he rightly emphasised the need for costly self-examination,[7] the vital place of prayer,[8] and the quality of the lives of Christians to support the preaching of the word. All these are necessary ingredients if we are serious about true revival. Even his description of the hallmarks of revival is almost unimprovable. It included: a conviction of sin among Christians and their repentance and renewal of faith, their love for others issuing in an evangelistic zeal, an appreciation of the reality of heaven accompanied by a loosening grip upon the world, and finally the salvation of many sinners.

However, the danger of his legacy is that Finney was fundamentally in error. His *Lectures on Theology*[9] reveal how far he differed from the 'reformed theology' of, for example, Jonathan Edwards whom he vigorously attacked. Finney's theology was thoroughly man-centred. He believed that we are not born into a state of sin (he denied 'original sin'), and that men and women therefore have 'a natural ability to obey God'.[10] He denied what Luther called 'the bondage of the will', and he denied the sovereign

> The danger of Finney's legacy is that he was fundamentally in error

initiative of God in election and the full security of believers (the final perseverance of the saints). For him justification was neither forensic nor judicial, nor (necessarily) eternal, and the righteousness of Christ was not imputed to the sinner. All these doctrines he declared to be 'better fitting

---

7 *Revivals of Religion—Lectures by Charles Grandison Finney*. Ed. with notes by William Henry Harding, (Marshall, Morgan and Scott, 1913), pp. 33–34. More accessible for today's reader is an edited edition by Bethany House Publishers, Minneapolis, 1988. However, my references are to the older edition. Iain Murray in *Revival and Revivalism* (Banner of Truth, 1994), also analyses Finney's theology and method, pp. 228–252.

8 Finney, *Revivals of Religion*, p. 49. Especially see Lecture 8 where he has some helpful advice for those who lead a prayer meeting.

9 See Finney's *Lectures on Theology* (Eerdmans, 1953). The lectures were originally given to the students at Oberlin College in America in 1846. The first publication in England was in 1851.

10 Above, p. 326.

a romance than a system of theology'.[11] In fact Finney used orthodox language to describe theology but invested much of it with a wholly new meaning—a meaning often peculiar to himself.

Significantly, Finney denied that conversion was the result of regeneration; rather it was the result of moral persuasion. This meant that he confused the author of any true spiritual work with the agent that God might use. Finney claimed that 'As an agent God works in two ways.' Those two ways were God's providential interference in circumstances and the direct influence of his Holy Spirit. That may appear orthodox until we realise that Finney thought of God as merely one agent among at least two others. The messenger is equally an agent as is the sinner himself. It is the entirely free interplay of each of these that may, or may not, achieve the salvation of the sinner. On the one hand Finney states clearly that Christians, 'must realise their complete dependence upon the Holy Spirit or their efforts will fail', but immediately adds, 'If Christians start to believe that God is necessary because sinners are *unable* to obey, or that God is obligated to give his Holy Spirit in order to make sinners able to obey the gospel, they insult God and their prayers will fail' (italics original).[12] This prepared the ground for his insistence that revivals can be induced by the employment of the correct techniques—he called them 'the constituted means'.

In 1832, two years before Finney first gave his lectures on this subject, William Sprague, a Presbyterian minister and graduate of Yale and Princeton, had published his own *Lectures on Revivals of Religion*. In it he used this same division of Providence and the Spirit. Finney was deliberately responding from his own perspective. Although Finney covered some of the same territory as Sprague, the two men came from very different theological perspectives. Whilst both men spoke of human

---

11 Above, p. 397.
12 *Lectures on Revival*, pp. 196–197.

responsibility, Sprague wrote of the 'agency of the Spirit in performing the change' in the sinner's heart.[13] That was an admission Finney would not make. For him, the Spirit could influence, but not accomplish the change.

Sprague also warned against 'substituting human inventions for divinely appointed means' and concluded, 'Brethren, we honour the Holy Spirit most, when we give him precisely the place which he claims; when we recognise him as the efficient author of conviction, conversion and sanctification; but he is offended when we undertake to palm upon him what we ought to take with shame to ourselves.'[14] Sprague also argued that the end does not justify the means, and that physical responses are not necessarily evidence of a spiritual conversion. Unquestionably the Princeton graduate was warning against the 'new measures' that Finney had been promoting for some years.

Finney entirely misrepresented, or perhaps he simply misunderstood, the theology of those he criticised. He maintained that the Reformed view of the sovereignty of God (represented by Sprague, and Jonathan Edwards before him) meant that we can only trust God and do nothing; and that the church has no more influence in producing a revival 'than in producing thunder, hail or an earthquake'. Sprague had actually used similar language himself,[15] but he knew that a true understanding of God's sovereignty has never taken a passive view. By confusing the author (God) with the agent (man), Finney was free virtually to dispense with the author and focus upon the activity of the agent. He condemned the idea that, 'Promoting religion is somehow so mysterious a subject of divine sovereignty, that there is no connection between the means and the end.' In fact, the Reformed theology that he so despised had never doubted that God is both God of the end and the means to the end.

---

13 William B. Sprague, *Lectures on Revivals of Religion* (Banner of Truth, 1959), p. 102.
14 Above, p. 112.
15 Above, p. 105.

Finney's theology of means and ends is stated simply: 'There is one fact under the government of God of universal notice and of everlasting remembrance which is, that the most useful and important things are most easily and certainly obtained by the use of the appropriate means.'[16] In other words, if the church does the right things, blessing (revival) will inevitably follow.

Whilst there is truth and value in many parts of his twenty-two lectures on revival, it was this man-centred approach that slowly formed the understanding of the word revival over much of the world. Finney was convinced that if the church meets the correct requirements then the desired result will inevitably follow: 'The law connecting cause and effect is more undeviating in spiritual than in natural things, and so there are fewer exceptions.'[17] He concluded that the only way for the church to advance is by periodic 'excitements' and that revival was not a miracle in the sense of 'Divine interference' but 'a purely philosophical result of the right use of the constituted means.'[18]

If the study of revival in North America had dealt justly with another preacher, who was arguably of even greater value than Finney, the present understanding might be better. Asahel Nettleton was almost ten years Finney's senior and he saw tens of thousands converted under his preaching. However, whilst Nettleton was a household name in America early in the nineteenth century, today he appears to be unknown to many books and exhibitions on the history of evangelism and revival on that continent.

Nettleton held a high view of the sovereignty of God and strongly opposed Finney's theology and methods. Nettleton was a man of passionate prayer and earnest preaching, yet he was convinced that both revival and regeneration were sovereign works of God, and that man should never

---

16 Finney, *Revivals of Religion*, p. 6.
17 Above, p. 29.
18 Above, p. 5.

dare to try to manipulate the work of the Spirit. He took issue with Finney but, weakened by typhus fever, he predeceased Finney by three decades and, although he established a seminary to train preachers, he left no lectures, no books, and few printed sermons. One of his biographers laments, 'By the turn of the twentieth century his name and life had fallen into oblivion.'[19] It was therefore left to Finney to dominate the American mind-set on the subject of revival to the present day. In the course of time revival, that Finney understood as the inevitable outcome of correct human endeavour, became synonymous with the enthusiastic endeavour itself.

In the sovereignty of God, Finney's methods did not hinder God from working in true revival across America and subsequently across large tracts of the world following the Fulton Street prayer meetings of 1857.[20] Nor did it hinder a real work of God among both Union and Confederate armies during the American Civil War. But it did leave the legacy that many have come to believe revivals can be 'worked up'. A widespread reading of the life of Nettleton, the lectures of Sprague and the works of Jonathan Edwards would re-establish a correct view of revival.[21]

Understanding revival

Revival, as conversion itself, is a sovereign act of God's grace and mercy, and not the result of any human effort or scheme. Both revival and conversion are not primarily the sinner coming to God, but God coming to the sinner. This must be emphasised, in the light of Finney's methodology.

---

19 J. F. Thornbury, *God Sent Revival* (Evangelical Press, 1977), p. 227.

20 The best contemporary record of the origins of this revival that led to the conversion of possibly one million people in America is found in Samuel Prime's, *The Power of Prayer* (Banner of Truth, 1991). Originally it was published in 1859 and Finney was quite disparaging of it.

21 Richard F. Lovelace in *Dynamics of Spiritual Life* (Inter-Varsity and Paternoster, 1979) writes, 'It is not too strong a statement to contend that the whole career of evangelicalism in America would have been cleansed of its distinctive scandals if Edwards had remained alive in the memory of the revivalists.' p. 243.

In revival, a deep conviction of sin is demanded and expected. It is acknowledged that there is no true conversion without this. It may lead to 'soul anguish' or 'penitential pain' as some have described it. However, an awakening to spiritual realities and a conviction of sin are *not* the same as conversion. This was a point well understood by Jonathan Edwards in his early eighteenth-century analysis of revival in New England. It was also constantly underlined by the Methodists in the same century. William Carvosso, who was significantly used in revival at Mousehole in Cornwall a century later, when over two hundred of the one thousand inhabitants became Christians, was at pains to stress this point; similarly, Duncan Campbell and most leaders in historic revivals.

True revival does not begin with happiness but with holiness, and holiness begins in tears. Holiness of life will and must follow as evidence for true revival.

In revival, Christianity becomes an experience of knowing God in Christ, admiring the beauty of Jesus, and sensing the presence of God. It is enjoying a full, unhindered appreciation of total forgiveness. Doubts fly away. The answer to Paul's prayer is fully experienced in times of revival:

> True revival does not begin with happiness but with holiness, and holiness begins in tears

'I pray that out of his glorious riches he may strengthen you with power through his Spirit in your inner being, so that Christ may dwell in your hearts through faith. And I pray that you, being rooted and established in love, may have power, together with all the saints, to grasp how wide and long and high and deep is the love of Christ, and to know this love that surpasses knowledge—that you may be filled to the measure of all the fulness of God' (Ephesians 3:16–19).

Chapter 1

Leaders in times of revival know that a faithful, godly, biblical ministry is not enough. It must be accompanied by a divine visitation. Revival is evidence of the ultimate triumph of God over Satan. Stuart Piggin has written, 'A revival is a manifestation in this world of a divine victory in a supernatural world.'[22] That should never be forgotten. It explains not only the supreme glory of transformed lives, both of believer and unbeliever, but the desperate attempts of Satan to destroy a revival by ungodly excess.

The wise acceptance that God is free to work in his own way in revival does not mean that anything goes. The relationship between the Spirit and the word must never be divorced. The Holy Spirit will not work in a way that is contrary to his own revelation in Scripture. One reason why the church in ordinary times needs to attend to sound doctrine (Titus 2:1) is so that the human excesses and errors, that so frequently slip into times of revival, will be identified and rejected—early and firmly.

Whilst God will never allow *us* to dictate the parameters of revival, he has certainly set his own; and some of these are clearly revealed in the Bible. However, Iain Murray makes the point: 'Those who have seen great revivals have been the first to say there was so much that left them amazed and conscious of mystery.'[23]

The word 'revival' is easier to describe than to define. When definitions are attempted, they generally refer to the preceding time of spiritual coldness, ineffectiveness or lethargy among the people of God. Generally, that is a fair assumption and certainly most of the biblical revivals reveal that.[24] On the other hand, it is not always true that the first work of the Spirit is to 'revive' a dying church. If Pentecost is seen as the revival to which the Old Testament prophets looked forward in longing, we must

22 'The Lord's Firestorms', Stuart Piggin in *The Evangelical Review of Theology*, Vol.23, No.3, July 1999.
23 Iain H. Murray, *Pentecost—Today?*, pp.5–6.
24 See *Revival—a people saturated with God*, chapter 4, pp.28–35.

not forget that on this occasion the Spirit worked first for the conversion of thousands of unsaved Jews and proselytes. Therefore, whilst the word 'revival' implies a 're-viving' of a life that is dying, we must not allow our word to preclude those occasions when God's chief purpose is to resurrect the dead. Unusual and atypical that may be, but then, revival is the unusual.

The Holy Spirit coming upon God's people, both in biblical history and in the subsequent history of the Christian church, reveals specific hallmarks that enable us to test the genuine from the counterfeit.

The *definition* of true revival offered in *Revival—a people saturated with God* is in itself a *description*:

Revival is a sovereign work of God's Holy Spirit resulting in an unusual awakening of spiritual life among God's people. This results in an awesome awareness of God, a deep conviction of sin, a longing for holiness, a renewed joy and love for the Father and the Son, and a passion to reach the lost. It is generally accompanied by a significant number of the lost coming to a true faith in Christ.[25]

However, we cannot improve on Duncan Campbell's descriptive phrase: 'A community saturated with God'. Revival is big, radical, unusual, always God initiated and always God honouring.

Neither geography nor brevity can be allowed to define a revival. Revival is not defined by where God does it or for how long. It cannot be measured by its location or its duration but by its intensity. The five hallmarks noted in the description above are discovered in both biblical and historic revivals and they describe revival

> Neither geography nor brevity can be allowed to define a revival. Revival is what God does, not where he does it or how long for

25 *Revival—a people saturated with God*, p. 22.

whether in one congregation for one month or in many communities for years.

Here are the five hallmarks again:

An awesome awareness of God

A deep conviction of sin

A longing for holiness

A renewed joy and love for the Father and the Son

A passion to reach the lost.

Preaching under the heading of 'What is revival?', C. H. Spurgeon reminded his nineteenth century congregation that not every Christian should always be crying for revival:

'Feeding and lying down in green pastures and led by the still waters, they ought not always to be crying, 'My leanness, my leanness, woe unto me!' Sustained by gracious promises and enriched out of the fullness which God has treasured up in his dear Son, their souls should prosper and be in health, and their piety ought to need no reviving. They should aspire to a higher blessing, a richer mercy, than a mere revival. They should be asking for growth in grace, for increase of strength, and for greater success.'[26]

For a man who believed passionately in revival, 'a mere revival' is a strange expression. Can there be anything more successful than revival? However, perhaps Spurgeon touches a vital note. A longing for revival should never steal us away from pressing on in our Christian life and experience to a greater holiness and closer walk with God. A cry for revival is not because we are dry, but because by being dry God and his Son Jesus Christ are not honoured.

The highest motive for a longing for revival is expressed in Isaiah 26:8: 'Yes, LORD, walking in the way of your laws, we wait for you; your name

26 C. H. Spurgeon, *The Sword and the Trowel*, December 1866.

and renown are the desire of our hearts.' Anything less is unworthy. God may satisfy our thirst and renew our zeal without necessarily giving revival. We must learn to be a people satisfied with God even when we are not yet saturated with God. A satisfied dissatisfaction is one of those necessary paradoxes of the Christian life. Revival should never be the all-consuming concern of the church. Good things

> We must learn to be a people satisfied with God even when we are not yet saturated with God

can happen for the church and through the church, even on the outside of revival. Both personally and corporately there is such a thing as a church renewed. The prayer meeting that insists on revival or nothing at all, is in grave danger of receiving nothing.

The nineteenth century Methodists believed that without periodic revivals the church would die. Finney, went further by claiming, 'Nothing but a revival of religion can prevent the means of grace from doing great injury to the ungodly. Without a revival they will grow harder and harder under preaching and will experience a more horrible damnation than they would if they had never heard the gospel.'[27] Even though overstated, there is some truth here. How many pastors lament members of their congregation becoming hardened and indifferent to the preaching? Typically, Finney overstated his conviction: 'Nothing but revival can preserve a church from annihilation.' That may be good rhetoric, but even with a heart-longing and theological commitment to revival, it is neither accurate nor helpful. There is renewal apart from revival. If God will not yet bring revival then he surely must want his people to be constantly renewed in heart, mind and spirit according to his word.

However, the plea in this book is that Christian people must and can pray for the big thing—a God-given revival.

---

27 Charles Finney, *Revivals of Religion*, p. 22.

2. The Holy Spirit in the Old Testament and Pentecost

Any discussion of the work of the Holy Spirit will confront Pentecost (Acts 2) as a crucial point in our understanding. Exactly what was the Holy Spirit doing throughout the Old Testament, and how does this compare and contrast with his work under the new covenant? What happened at Pentecost is the key to that question. But first, it is wise to have a firm understanding of the work of the Spirit under the old covenant.

Some suggest that we cannot properly use 'revival' to refer to anything that happened in the Old Testament because even though the verb is used many times (eg Psalm 80:18; 85:6), the noun 'revival' is not. However, the noun 'justification' is not found in the Old Testament to refer to our relationship with God, yet both Paul and James had no hesitation in using the verb 'justified' to refer to Abraham (Romans 4:2; James 2:24).

All aspects of the Spirit's ministry are found under the old covenant.

The Spirit in creation and the presence of God

In an unspecified way the Spirit was active at the time of Creation (Genesis 1:2), which means that at the dawning of history the Spirit is seen as the executive of God or, as the Princeton theologian Benjamin Warfield expressed it, the Spirit is the 'immanence of the transcendent God'.[28]

---

28 Benjamin B. Warfield, *Biblical and Theological Studies* (Presbyterian and Reformed Publishing Company, 1952), p. 134.

In less theological terms, that is precisely how our Lord promised the presence of the Spirit to his disciples: 'I will ask the Father, and he will give you another Counsellor to be with you for ever—the Spirit of truth … If anyone loves me … My Father will love him, and we will come to him and make our home with him' (John 14:16, 23).

Under the old covenant, the Spirit is understood as the omnipresence of God in this world. David had no doubt of the involvement of the Spirit of God in the events of the world and in his own life: 'Where can I go from your Spirit or where can I flee from your presence?' (Psalm 139:7). When David cried out in repentant fear: 'Do not cast me from your presence or take your Holy Spirit from me' (Psalm 51:11), he must have been aware of the presence of the Spirit in his life. Similarly, when Isaiah reflected on the presence of God in the history of Israel, this is how he described it: 'Where is he who set his Holy Spirit among them, who sent his glorious arm of power to be at Moses' right hand…?' (Isaiah 63:11–12).

The Spirit for prophecy and revelation

At the appointment of the seventy elders who were set apart to help Moses in leading the Israelites in the wilderness, God 'took of the Spirit that was on him [Moses] and put the Spirit on the seventy elders'; the result was that the men prophesied (Numbers 11:25). There is here a similarity with what happened at Ephesus fifteen hundred years later: 'Paul placed his hands on them, the Holy Spirit came on them, and they spoke in tongues and prophesied' (Acts 19:6). Similarly, Joshua is described as 'a man in whom is the Spirit' (Numbers 27:18), just as Stephen in Acts 6:5 was described as 'a man full of faith and of the Holy Spirit'.

When Jesus promised his disciples that the Spirit would 'teach you all things and bring to your remembrance all things that I said to you' (John 14:26), this was not a new concept. Five hundred years earlier, Nehemiah attributed the teaching of Moses to the work of the Holy Spirit: 'You gave your good Spirit to instruct them [Israel]' (Nehemiah 9:20), and so it was throughout the centuries that followed: 'For many years ... you testified against them by your Spirit in your prophets' (9:30). Isaiah even thought of the Spirit as one who could be grieved, 'They rebelled and grieved his Holy Spirit...' (Isaiah 63:10). This is an unmistakable parallel to Ephesians 4:30, 'And do not grieve the Holy Spirit of God.'

In the New Testament, Peter was aware that the Holy Spirit moved the Old Testament prophets: 'Holy men of God spoke as they were moved by the Holy Spirit' (2 Peter 1:21); but almost a millennium earlier David was aware of it also: 'The Spirit of the LORD spoke by me, and his word was on my tongue' (2 Samuel 23:2). This comparison between the Old and new covenants can be made scores of times.

The Spirit and gifts for service

The first clear example of the gift of the Spirit for service comes in the help that God gave to Moses so that he did not have to bear alone the responsibility of caring for the Israelites: 'I will take of the Spirit that is upon you and will put the same upon them' (Numbers 11:17, 25). Joshua was similarly divinely aided by the Spirit in his work and is described as 'a man in whom is the Spirit' (Numbers 27:18).

When specific work was to be undertaken for the Tabernacle, God equipped men in a way remarkably similar to the dispensing of gifts in the New Testament. Of Bezalel God said to Moses: 'See I have filled him with the Spirit of God, in wisdom, in understanding, in knowledge, and in all manner of workmanship with skill, ability and knowledge in all kinds of crafts...' (Exodus 31:3; 35:31). Half a millennium later the same Spirit revealed the plans of the Temple to David: 'David gave his son Solomon ... the plans of all that he had [received] by the Spirit' (1 Chronicles 28:11–12). The parallel is evident in 1 Corinthians 12:4, 7, 'There are different kinds of gifts, but the same Spirit ... To each one the manifestation of the Spirit is given for the common good.'

This theme is followed throughout the book of Judges and beyond. The Spirit was essential for the service of God. Even the experience of Philip in Acts 8:39, 'The Spirit of the Lord caught Philip away…' is paralleled in Ezekiel 11:1, 'Then the Spirit lifted me up and brought me to the east gate of the LORD's house.'

Once again, these are examples of many more.

The Spirit for filling and regeneration

The phrase 'filled with the Spirit' is not confined to the post-Pentecost experience. Both Elizabeth and Zechariah were 'filled with the Holy Spirit (Luke 1:41, 67). Joshua, who took over the leadership of Israel from Moses, was 'filled with the Spirit of wisdom' (Deuteronomy 34:9). Bezalel was 'filled … with the Spirit of God, with skill, ability and knowledge…' (Exodus 31:3). Proverbs uses the idea of the Spirit of wisdom being 'poured out' upon those who will turn at wisdom's rebuke (1:23). In this sense Micah claimed to be 'filled with power, with the Spirit of the LORD' (Micah 3:8).

The Spirit has always been essential for anyone to seek and find God. The announcement: 'At that time men began to call on the name of the LORD' (Genesis 4:26) and the subsequent warning that 'My Spirit will not contend with man for ever' (Genesis 6:3) are evidence of the Spirit at work in the conviction of sin. This is the same Holy Spirit of whom the apostle wrote in the New Testament, 'No- one can say, "Jesus is Lord," except by the Holy Spirit' (1 Corinthians 12:3). When Abraham was called to serve the true God and abandon his pagan worship of the moon-god in Ur of the Chaldeans, he needed a work of the Holy Spirit in his life no less than Saul of Tarsus two millennia later. That work can only be described as the 'new birth' referred to in John 3:3, Titus 3:5 and 1 Peter 1:23 for example. Our theological term is 'regeneration'.

A warning: The attempt to distinguish between the Old Testament when the Spirit came 'upon' men, and the New when he came 'into' them, cannot be upheld. Phrases such as 'in whom is the Spirit' (Numbers 27:18), and 'filled … with the Spirit' (Exodus 31:3), whilst not common, are too frequent to be dismissed. It is not wise to make a hard distinction in the Old Testament between the use of the Hebrew prepositions *al* meaning 'on' (Numbers 11:25) and *beth* meaning 'in' (Numbers 27:18). Just as it is not wise in the New Testament to make a hard distinction between the Greek *en* meaning 'in' (John 14:17) and *epi* meaning 'upon' (Acts 1:8). How would we resolve the fact that the Spirit was *in* Joshua (Numbers 27:18) but he came *on* the young disciples at Ephesus (Acts 19:6), or that God promised to put his Spirit *upon* Christ (Matthew 12:18, see also 3:16)? If we insist that after Pentecost the Spirit, who is within the people of God (John 14:17) comes upon them for particular occasions (Acts 19:6), exactly the same could be said of the Old Testament when we compare Numbers 27:18 with 11:25.

It is never wise to build a theology upon prepositions!

> It is never wise to build a theology upon prepositions!

The Spirit for sanctification

The use of the word 'holy' to designate the Spirit, is not confined to the new covenant. Although it is not common, we find it in Psalm 51:11 and Isaiah 63:10–11. Elsewhere the psalmist acknowledges, 'May your good Spirit lead me on level ground' (Psalm 143:10). It is this work in sanctifying the people of God that is most frequent in the Old Testament.

When the prophet Ezekiel condemned the nation of Israel for its rebellion against God, a rebellion which had led to the exile, he also prophesied of a day coming when Israel would be returned to its own land. This was fulfilled at the time of the decree of Cyrus, king of Persia, in 539 BC (Ezra 1:1–4). At the same time Ezekiel promised that Israel would return as a sanctified people:

'I will gather you from all the countries and bring you back into your own land. I will sprinkle clean water on you, and you will be clean; I will cleanse you from all your impurities and from all your idols. I will give you a new heart and put a new spirit in you; I will remove from you your heart of stone and give you a heart of flesh. And I will put my Spirit in you and move you to follow my decrees and be careful to keep my laws' (Ezekiel 36:24–27).

The words that he employed for this new spiritual life focused even more on the work of the Spirit than those used when Jeremiah outlined the benefits of the post-Pentecost new covenant (Jeremiah 31:33).

The psalms are beautiful pictures of adoration and the enjoyment of God with which new covenant believers can readily identify. The work of the Spirit in the Old Testament included personal transformation both morally and spiritually, hence David's plea for a 'pure heart' and a 'steadfast spirit' in the context of his fear of losing 'your Holy Spirit' (Psalm 51:10–11).

In our attempt to magnify the work of God under the new covenant, we often overlook how much was experienced under the Old. The New Testament writers were aware of the depth of spiritual experience enjoyed by their fathers in the faith. The Jews in the first century who heard Jesus or read the apostles would certainly not have been mystified by their teaching about the Holy Spirit. There were too many references to the Spirit in their Hebrew Scriptures for them to miss the continuation of his ministry. Benjamin Warfield, the Princeton theologian of the late nineteenth and early twentieth centuries, goes so far as to claim, 'In passing from the Old Testament to the New, the reader is conscious of no violent discontinuity in the conception of the Spirit which he finds in the two volumes.'[29]

---

29 Benjamin B. Warfield, *Biblical and Theological Studies*, p. 128

What is the distinction between the old covenant and Pentecost?

Any understanding of the work of the Spirit cannot avoid the fact that Pentecost introduced something new and dramatic. There is 'no violent discontinuity' in his work, but here is nevertheless something significantly more.

A NEW *UNDERSTANDING* OF THE SPIRIT'S WORK

Whilst the Holy Spirit was active throughout the Old Testament—in creation, regeneration, equipping and supplying gifts for service, in the revelation of Scripture and prophesy, and in revival—there was a significant lack of understanding of who he was. There are aspects of the person and work of the Spirit that require the revelation of the New Testament.

When Paul met the new Christian converts in Ephesus and asked them if they had received the Holy Spirit when they believed (Acts 19:2), it is doubtful whether their response confused him as much as it has confused generations of commentators. Their reply: 'We have not so much as heard whether there is a Holy Spirit', was not surprising. Little was written by the Jews about the Holy Spirit during the almost half a millennium from Malachi to Matthew. Throughout this period, although the Qumran scrolls do refer to the Spirit, they reveal no doctrine of a personal Spirit, and they contain no equivalent word for the wonderful New Testament term 'paraclete'.

There is no overt reference to the Spirit of God in at least half the books of the Old Testament, and in the fifty-two chapters of the prophet Jeremiah, the Spirit is not directly referred to once. Significantly, when Jeremiah expounds on the new covenant in glowing language being written 'on their hearts' (31:31–34) he never explicitly casts it in terms of the Spirit, even though Paul is ready to apply that to the newly converted Corinthians as a reference to the 'Spirit of the living God' (2 Corinthians 3:3), and distinctly claims that the new covenant is a covenant of the Spirit (2 Corinthians 3:6).

When Jesus responded to Nicodemus: 'You are Israel's teacher, and do you not understand these things?' (John 3:10) he was challenging Nicodemus to be ready for a fuller understanding of the work of the Spirit. Teacher of Israel he may be, but the day had arrived when all the Lord's people would understand more than he did. The question was therefore rhetorical; it was designed to draw the enquirer's enquiry even further.

A NEW *EXPERIENCE* OF THE SPIRIT'S PRESENCE

The Old Testament prepares the people for an outpouring of the Spirit. Although the expression, 'I will pour out my Spirit' occurs only four times (Isaiah 44:3; Ezekiel 39:29; Joel 2:28–29; and possibly Proverbs 1:23), the preparation for this experience was there in Ezekiel 37, Isaiah 44:3, and Joel 2:28.

When John the Baptist introduced the Messiah as 'The one whom God ... gives the Spirit without limit' (John 3:34), there is more than a hint that up until this point God's Spirit had been given with constraint. At the least it must mean that his work will not be limited to Israel but will be given to people from all nations. In this way we can understand John 7:39: 'Up to that time the Spirit had not been given, since Jesus had not yet been glorified.' Similarly, when Jesus breathed on his disciples and promised, 'Receive the Holy Spirit' (John 20:22), it was a symbolic act pointing to the forthcoming Pentecost. It is certain that these men were regenerate already and that the Spirit therefore indwelt them. Jesus was now preparing them for a greater experience of initiation.

Jesus instructed his disciples concerning the work of the Spirit in the individual—convicting of sin, righteousness and judgement (John 16:8)—and this was more than simply drawing back the veil on what the Spirit's work had always been. The Spirit had always been active like this, but the disciples would experience something more. There would be a personal experience of the Spirit unknown to most of the faithful before. A few under the old covenant could experience this because God's grace allowed them an experience under the law as if they were under the new covenant. Similarly, David experienced forgiveness for a sin that could not be atoned for under the law (2 Samuel 12:13; compare Leviticus 20:10), and his psalms reveal a warm, deep and passionate love for God. However, Pentecost provided such an outpouring of the Spirit that all new covenant believers can experience the personal reality of God in their lives in a way that only a few did under the old covenant.

Faithful believers under the old covenant saw themselves primarily in the community of the people of God who belonged to the land of Israel. The nationhood of Israel was as much associated with the land (and later the temple) as it was associated with their covenant with God; the two were inseparable. Religion and state, geography and nationhood were indistinguishable.

Pentecost changed this. The temple and land became wholly irrelevant to the Christian community. Part of the symbol of the tongues of fire was that God now dwelt within all disciples of Christ so that each became a temple of the Spirit (1 Corinthians 6:19) and together they are built into a holy temple (Ephesians 2:21–22). The visible symbols of the presence of God among his people Israel—the cloud and temple—would be gone for ever, and the invisible, indwelling Holy Spirit would be the presence of Christ among his people. This is the major significance of our Lord's teaching in John 14 to 16.

The new covenant experience of the Spirit also taught adoption as a personal experience and not as a national association. The concept of God as a Father of the individual was almost unknown under the old covenant; his Fatherhood was for the nation (Jeremiah 3:4). Paul introduced the radically new emphasis of personal adoption (Romans 8:14–16). Under the old covenant, adoption was through membership of the community of Israel; under the new covenant membership of the new Israel (the church) is by the Spirit's personal adoption and God becomes the Father of every believer.

Western Christianity is sometimes accused of ignoring the biblical significance of community; however, we must not return to the Old Testament concept that community is all. The Spirit came to make the experience of individual faith very real. That is a significant discontinuity between the two testaments.

In the Old Testament the experience of Bezalel (Exodus 31:1–3) was exceptional; now, however, 'The manifestation of the Spirit is given to each one for the common good' (1 Corinthians 12:7). Gifts are given by the personal intervention of the Holy Spirit to all the Lord's people, not only to a select few.

The concepts of 'being filled with the Spirit' and of being 'baptized in the Spirit' clearly have a new dynamic under the new covenant. We have already seen that the presence of the Spirit coming powerfully upon men in the Old Testament is not entirely absent; however, it was exceptional and not commonplace. The vision given to Ezekiel in the valley of bones, together with the promise: 'I will put my Spirit in you, and you shall live' (Ezekiel 37:14), was directed to the corporate life of Israel. In the New Testament the entire company of Christians were filled with the Spirit repeatedly and individually (e.g. Acts 4:31).

Today, Christians too often live as if they were under the old covenant. Their faith is impersonal and could hardly be described as 'dynamic'. The individual relies heavily upon the society of the church, and few Western Christians would maintain a healthy relationship with God if they were denied access to their Christian community. We are often incapable of counselling ourselves from the Scriptures: requiring professional counsellors to resolve our emotions, and professional teachers to answer our questions. Revival is an experience

> Revival is an experience by which the Spirit draws the church away from its backsliding into the Old Testament and re-creates a New Testament experience

by which the Spirit draws the church away from its backsliding into the Old Testament and re-creates a New Testament experience.

A NEW *COMMISSION* BY THE SPIRIT'S AUTHORITY

Pentecost heralded a universal gospel for the whole world. Every true believer is privileged to act as prophet. When the Holy Spirit came down upon the Christians at Pentecost they were commissioned and anointed to do what only a few prophets had been called to do through the centuries of the Old Testament. Now, merchants, civil servants and soldiers are ambassadors for Christ. For the first time, Moses' longing recorded in Numbers 11:29 was fulfilled: 'I wish that all the LORD's people were prophets and the LORD would put his Spirit on them.'

Peter claimed the fulfilment of Joel 2:28–29,32 at Pentecost (Acts 2:18,21). However, the vital part of Joel's promise is the point at which Peter stops in his quotation: the end is that 'Everyone who calls on the name of the LORD will be saved.' This is the universal offer of the gospel.

Prophecy—telling God's message—is no longer the preserve of a few but the privilege of all. The tongues of fire symbolized the pouring out of the Spirit for those from every part of the Roman Empire and beyond. The gift of speaking in their diverse languages (tongues) was God's seal that he was sending his message to the whole world and that all his people were now prophets proclaiming the message without distinction of Jew or Gentile.

In this sense the 'Samaritan Pentecost' (Acts 8:14–17) and the 'Gentile Pentecost' (Acts 10:44–46 and compare Peter's comment in 11:15) were even more radical events than the Jewish Pentecost. Nothing like this had happened since the passing phenomenon of the days of Jonah. This was now to be permanent. Jewish pilgrims from what today is Iran, Iraq, Syria, Palestine, Turkey, Armenia, Egypt, Libya, Italy, Crete, Jordan and Lebanon, returned to their homes filled with the Spirit, to declare 'the wonders of God'. No longer were they 'God-fearing Jews from every nation under heaven' (Acts 2:5) jealously guarding the faith in their synagogues, they were now disciples of Christ with a world-wide evangelistic mission. This prophetic ministry was now the task of every believer. A new era of the Spirit's work had dawned.

A NEW *AUTHORITY* BY THE SPIRIT'S POWER

Jesus promised his disciples that they would receive 'power when the Holy Spirit comes on you' (Acts 1:8). This was the opening of a new chapter in the work of the Spirit, and it would enable them to fulfil their new commission. The promise of power was not primarily for a flurry of miracles that would prove to be 'signs of an apostle' (2 Corinthians 12:12), nor even for the rarely repeated gift of speaking in languages unknown to the speaker (Acts 2, 10, 19). The real evidence of the power of the Spirit is seen in the authority of God's word and the testimony of changed lives. The church has grown over the succeeding two millennia not through 'miracles and wonders' but through the Spirit working through the word of God and the transformed lives of those converted to Christ.

Paul placed his confidence in 'a demonstration of the Spirit's power' which he defined as 'My message and my preaching' (1 Corinthians 2:4). In consequence of this, lives were changed, and Paul could commend the Corinthians for the fact that 'You yourselves are our letter … known and read by everybody' (2 Corinthians 3:2). When Israel was intended to be a witness to the nations (Deuteronomy 4:5–8), it was the nation, not the individual, that was in view. The New Testament focus is always upon the transformation of the individual so that the corporate witness of the church will be effective.

The 'greater works' promised by our Lord to all who believe in him (John 14:12) have been too often misunderstood. No individual has ever equalled, let alone exceeded, the miracles of Christ. The purpose of the supernatural in our Lord's life was to demonstrate his divine authority as the Son of God (John 14:11). However, the greatest thing that he had been doing was preaching the Kingdom of God to 'the lost sheep of the house of Israel' (Matthew 15:24). In John 14 the disciples were promised that all who have faith in him will do far greater things, and this refers to the universal mission of the church after Pentecost. In the context of John 14, our Lord immediately went on to give his disciples the most detailed teaching on the promised coming of the Spirit that they would ever receive (John 14 to 17).

The promise by Jesus of the gift of the Holy Spirit was in the context of their new commission. Thus the 'Counsellor' will be sent to the disciples so that the world will be convinced of sin, righteousness and judgement (John 16:8). Similarly, when Christ breathed on the disciples and said, 'Receive the Holy Spirit' (John 20:22), he immediately placed this action in the context of their gospel ministry: 'As the Father has sent me, I am sending you.' The same is true in Acts 1:8. The power of the Spirit is given to the disciples of Christ so that they might exercise, not only the prophetic ministry, but the prophetic authority. The gospel, through the Spirit, is the power of God for salvation to everyone who believes, and every Christian carries that authority.

Conclusion

When we are speaking of the contrasting work of the Spirit between the old and new covenants, we should not speak of degree or kind, but of dynamic and purpose, or perhaps better still—potential. That word carries the idea of a capability or purpose that is latent, waiting for the fullness of time before being fully unleashed—exactly as forgiveness, justification and reconciliation only reach their fullness under the new covenant. The Spirit gave himself to his people in the Old Testament, but with a more limited purpose in view, and therefore with restraint. Consequently, whilst there was undoubtedly revival in the time of Hezekiah, it did not have the fullness and dynamic that we find in the New Testament and beyond.

Under the old covenant the Spirit was at work both in the individual and in the community and the marks of his activity can be seen in conviction, regeneration and revival. However, he limited his potential until the time had fully come, and at Pentecost the Spirit came upon the people of God in a universal outpouring for a universal purpose, so that with a new understanding, experience, commission and authority they might win the world for Jesus.

> At Pentecost the Spirit came upon the people of God in a universal outpouring for a universal purpose, so that with a new understanding, experience, commission and authority they might win the world for Jesus

3. Examples of revival in the Old Testament

Throughout the Old Testament there were clearly times when, from a time of backsliding and disobedience, the people returned toward God with new life. When Paul informed the Christians at Rome that 'everything that was written in the past was written to teach us' (Romans 15:4) he must have intended that these occasions were to teach us something of God's purpose for his people when they are in spiritual lethargy or worse.

Some writers on this subject accept that there are prophecies of revival in the Old Testament but insist that it is wrong to look for the experience of revival there.[30] However, we have seen in the previous chapter there is an important continuity between the Old and New Testaments. Whilst acknowledging that it may not be seen in the fullness of the new covenant experience, revival is part of that continuity. It will be helpful to identify a few of the more significant occasions in the history of Israel when revival may be presumed or explicitly seen.

From Creation to the wilderness

Throughout the story of God's people in the Old Testament there is a tragic cycle of spiritual decline and spiritual restoration both personally and nationally. The first example of this is to be found in Genesis 4:26 with the simple statement: 'Then men began to call on the name of the Lord.' Although we cannot know exactly what happened at this time, there is a clear implication that from the fall of Adam there was a steady decline

---

30 The position of Iain H. Murray in *Pentecost—Today?* (Banner of Truth, 1998). p. 16.

until the position had been reached where his descendants were no longer calling upon God.

Seth stands in marked contrast to the prevailing and violent arrogance of Lamech and the descendants of Cain (Genesis 4:23–24). The Hebrew scholar Keil came close to the reality when he commented, 'While the family of the Cainites, by the erection of a city and the invention and development of worldly arts and business, were laying the foundation for the kingdom of this world, the family of the Sethites began, by united invocation of the name of the God of grace, to found and erect the kingdom of God.'[31]

It is generally accepted that the form of the Hebrew strongly implies that from this time on men 'used the name of the LORD (Yahweh) in worship'. This would therefore be the first notice in Scripture that the character of God as the LORD was recognized and worshipped by fallen humanity. It is a matter of debate how far Seth and his family used the covenant name of God simply as the means of access to him and how far they understood the character of God that was revealed in that name (see Exodus 3:13–15, and 6:2–4). However, what is clear is that a radical turning point in the division of the human race had begun.

Many commentators see this as the commencement of public worship, as opposed to the private worship of God.[32] Calvin goes so far as to suggest that at this point in history: 'The face of the church began distinctly to appear.' He even compares it to the events of his own day in the sixteenth century: 'Such a restoration of religion has been effected also in our time.' Whether or not this is pressing the account too far, it is clear that from this time on, some people publicly called on the true God and some, sadly most, did not. This shift can be explained only in terms of a new and powerful work of God by his Spirit. Anything less does scant justice to the

---

31 Keil and Delitzsch, *Commentary on the Old Testament*, Vol. 1, p. 120.
32 For example Calvin, Keil and Delitzsch, Leupold, and Morris.

importance of this verse in Scripture. Unfortunately, it did not last, but the effect of that spiritual revival was decisive for the future of the human race because Noah, from the line of Seth, was a descendant of revival and he and his family alone survived the global Flood.[33]

From the Flood to the years of the Patriarchs we follow the story of one family through Abraham, Isaac and Jacob. The spiritual focus is narrowed to the lives of these men, and little is known of the religious commitment of their families or of the wider circle of their servants. All three men knew periods of backsliding and restoration, although that is not revival. Then, for more than four hundred years the Israelites suffered in Egypt. During this time their spiritual life was undoubtedly affected, as is evidenced by their eager return to the idols of Egypt (Exodus 32). Their cry for help recorded in Exodus 2:23–24 implies a time of spiritual revival, although what led to it, apart from an ever-increasing burden of slavery, we are not told. Their subsequent enthusiastic: 'We will do everything the LORD has said; we will obey' (Exodus 24:7) was sadly short-lived.

From Canaan to the monarchy

The generation that had grown up in the wilderness similarly pledged loyalty to Joshua and the word of the LORD (Joshua 1:16–18), and the preparation for the conquest bears the marks of a people who were serious with God. According to Nehemiah 8:17 the celebration of the Feast of Tabernacles at the return from exile, a thousand years after the Exodus, had never been celebrated with such joy and enthusiasm: 'their joy was very great.' If there is evidence of a true work of the Spirit under Nehemiah it must say the same for the time of Joshua.

After the death of Joshua and his Elders (Judges 2:7), the people continued in the momentum of revival but with an ever-evaporating zeal:

---

33 Although not all commentators would agree that Genesis 4:26 is revival, Jonathan Edwards and Andrew Bonar did.

'When all that generation had been gathered to their fathers, another generation arose after them who did not know the Lord nor the work which he had done for Israel. Then the children of Israel did evil in the sight of the Lord and served the Baals; and they forsook the Lord God of their fathers, who had brought them out of the land of Egypt … and they provoked the Lord to anger.'

Throughout the book of Judges we have a tragic cycle of events for nearly three hundred years: disobedience, disgrace, distress, repentance and deliverance. Thirteen times in the book of Judges that cycle is repeated. Judges 21:25 closes with the words 'everyone did what was right in his own eyes.' This was the dark age of Israel.

2 Chronicles 15:3–6 presents an alarming summary of those three hundred years of the Judges: 'For a long time Israel was without the true God, without a priest to teach and without the law. But in their distress they turned to the LORD, the God of Israel, and sought him, and he was found by them.' When the people cried to God, he came to them in deliverance. That deliverance does not bear all the hallmarks of New Testament revival, but perhaps it was a precursor to what we later learn.

We might suggest that many more periods of revival are hidden in the book of the Judges, and that without these the nation would have sunk permanently into the degenerate paganism of the surrounding nations. To take only one example: the cry of repentance as Jephthah came to power certainly reveals a true spiritual awakening. Together the people confessed their sin and threw themselves utterly on the mercy of God: 'We have sinned! Do to us whatever seems best to you; only deliver us this day, we pray' (Judges 10:15–16). Their active response in destroying the idols and serving the Lord clearly moved him to act for them. In the light of the terrible spiritual and moral condition, the fact that 'the Israelites cried out to the LORD', can perhaps only be understood as a spiritual revival. The 'Angel of the LORD ' is referred to twenty-one times in Judges, which is more than in any other Old Testament book. Where sin reigned in such terrifying darkness, grace was always present.

When Samuel began his public ministry, the nation had not seen spiritual revival since the days of Jephthah, more than one hundred years earlier. Samuel's powerful leadership was undoubtedly a time of new spiritual life for Israel. As he moved around his preaching circuit from Bethel to Gilgal to Mizpah to Ramah, the Lord 'let none of his words fall to the ground' (1 Samuel 3:19). Samuel's prophetic ministry was powerfully effective and revival began with the people's sincere repentance: 'All the people of Israel mourned and sought after the LORD' (1 Samuel 7:2). That it was true spiritual revival is evident from Samuel's assessment: 'If you are returning to the LORD with all your hearts…' (7:3). It was a heart-returning, supported by a significant change in their worship and behaviour: 'The Israelites put away the Baals and Ashtoreths, and served the LORD only' (7:4). Here we have an Old Testament example of the effective ministry of God's word leading to deep heartfelt repentance. Those two things, the power of God's word and true repentance, are significant marks of spiritual revival.

The kings of Judah

Saul squandered the spiritual gains of Samuel, and the first monarchy ended in unrelieved tragedy. David brought new life and hope to the nation. His own personal spiritual life, despite his sin over Bathsheba and Uriah, is revealed through the psalms attributed to him. David led the people spiritually and positively, but there is no record of widespread national revival during his reign. The fact that there are psalms appealing for revival may imply that much of the spiritual health of the nation at this time depended on the forceful leadership of David himself.

The same is probably true of Solomon who undoubtedly believed in God as a spiritually restoring God (1 Kings 8:33–53). However, since the general level of the nation's spiritual awareness was high during the rule of this wise king, there was little call for national revival. Revival is most frequently a sovereign work of God's Spirit after a period of spiritual coldness. An indication of the high level of spiritual life among the people at the time of Solomon's dedication of the temple is seen also in 1 Kings 8:66, '[Solomon] sent the people away; and they blessed the king, and went to their tents joyful and glad of heart for all the good that the LORD had done for his servant David, and for Israel his people.' If Psalm 72 is David's prayer for his successor, a prayer that God amply fulfilled, then the nation's spiritual life under Solomon was clearly at a high point.

At the division of the land during Rehoboam's reign in 931 BC, Jeroboam I established a monarchy over the northern kingdom of Israel. Among the twenty kings in the north, until Assyria finally defeated Samaria in 722 BC, there was not one good king. Our attention is directed towards the kingdom of Judah in the south because from there the line of the Messiah would come. The southern kingdom continued until the Babylonian captivity in 587 BC. Among the twenty kings in Judah were some outstandingly spiritual men: Asa, Jehoshaphat, Hezekiah and Josiah.

One objection that is sometimes levelled against the idea of spiritual revival during the monarchy is the fact that in those days of all-powerful rulers, a spiritual king did not require a spiritual people to achieve spiritual objectives. He could create changes simply by giving an order. That is true, and for this reason, we may think of the changes under Josiah as reformation rather than revival, because the changes came from the top and there is little clear indication of spiritual life among the people. However, the spiritual events during the days of Asa, Jehoshaphat and particularly Hezekiah, reveal something different. Changes were not the result merely of a royal decree. We are specifically told that the people were in favour of reform with their heart and soul. The changes were for a widespread spiritual transformation.

According to 2 Chronicles 15:17 Asa's heart 'was fully committed to the LORD all his life'. But the fact that it became a people's movement is clear from 2 Chronicles 15:12, '[The people] entered into a covenant to seek the LORD, the God of their fathers, with all their heart and soul', and also from verse 15, 'All Judah rejoiced about the oath because they had sworn it wholeheartedly.' Of the forty-one years of Asa's reign, revival continued for thirty-six of them. Revival is always a people's movement.

The same was true in Jehoshaphat's time: 'His heart took delight in the ways of the LORD' (2 Chronicles 17:6). This held true for twenty-five years during which time 'Jehoshaphat lived in Jerusalem, and he went out among the people from Beersheba [the southern border] to the hill country of Ephraim [the northern border] and turned them back to the LORD, the God of their fathers' (2 Chronicles 19:4) and 'The people of Judah came together to seek help from the LORD; indeed, they came from every town in Judah to seek him' (2 Chronicles 20:4). Here is a widespread, national response that can only be explained in terms of spiritual revival. 2 Chronicles 19:4 literally reads, 'he went out *again* among the people'. This must refer back to the officials who, in the third year of his reign taught 'the Book of the Law of the LORD' throughout Judah (2 Chronicles 17:7–9). The effect at that time was so powerful that 'the fear of the LORD' touched surrounding nations and the Philistines and Arabs brought unsolicited gifts to Jerusalem (17:10–11). Is this a distant echo of Acts 2:5–12?

Revival during the time of Hezekiah formed the biblical foundation for *Revival—a people saturated with God*.[34] Therefore, a summary is sufficient here. During this revival we find everything associated with revival: the presence of God, urgency, preaching, conviction of sin and repentance, sincere prayer, joyful worship, holiness of life and

---

34 Brian Edwards, *Revival—a people saturated with God* (Day One Publications, Leominster UK 2019).

evangelism. 'Hezekiah and all the people rejoiced at what God had brought about for his people' (2 Chronicles 29:36), and 'The hand of God was on the people to give them unity of mind to carry out what the king and his officials has ordered, following the word of the LORD' (2 Chronicles 30:12).

There can be no doubt that these three examples during the monarchy of Judah were powerful movements of God to revive the spiritual life of his people at a time when the knowledge of God had been almost eclipsed by the power of pagan religion. A king can change the people's activity, but he cannot change their hearts.

> A king can change the people's activity, but he cannot change their hearts

Before we leave the period of the monarchy we must turn to the remarkable events in the city of Nineveh, the capital of the Assyrian empire. Jonah was a prophet during the reigns of Jeroboam II in Israel and Amaziah in Judah. Jeroboam was an evil king (1 Kings 14:9) and Amaziah, who began well enough, soon 'turned away from following the LORD' (2 Chronicles 25:27). The spiritual life of the nation, both north and south, was at a low ebb. God sent Jonah away from Israel and Judah to a pagan nation. What happened in Nineveh was not a reviving of the spiritual life of God's people, but it was certainly a great outpouring of the Holy Spirit to change the hearts of 120,000 people in a pagan city. God by-passed his own people and sent his Spirit to a godless nation to bring a whole generation to repentance. This was a forerunner of what Paul referred to in Romans 11:11, 'Salvation has come to the Gentiles to make Israel envious.' It certainly had that effect in the life of Jonah! If we are to take the story of Jonah seriously, and Luke 11:32 compels us to, we must conclude that it is an account of a sudden and powerful work of the Holy Spirit in an unexpected place and with exceptional results.

After the Exile

In 587 BC Judah was taken into seventy years of Babylonian exile. The nation became a scattered, demoralized, and leaderless people. They were faced with a struggle for sheer spiritual survival. In Psalm 137 we can hear how the nations mocked them.

Rescue came as God said it would, through a royal decree of Cyrus, king of Persia. It was not only that God brought the people back from exile by a decree of a pagan king, but he turned the hearts of many of the people towards himself so that they wanted to come back. Psalm 126 reveals this: 'When the LORD brought back the captives to Zion, we were like men who dreamed. Our mouths were filled with laughter, our tongues with songs of joy.' Even though not all returned, in the light of the spiritual condition of the people who went into exile and the following decades of darkness which followed, that was revival.

This is described in the records of Ezra and Nehemiah. The walls of Jerusalem and the temple were rebuilt, but much more than this was accomplished. The events of those two books are mingled with waves of periodic revival as the various groups of exiles returned. When the zeal of the people cooled, the prophets Haggai and Zechariah, and later Malachi, were sent to rekindle their faith. What happened under the preaching of Haggai is recorded in Haggai 1:14, 'The LORD stirred up the spirit of Zerubbabel son of Shealtiel, governor of Judah, and the spirit of Joshua son of Jehozadak, the high priest, and the spirit of the whole remnant of the people.'

The joy and weeping recorded in Ezra 3:13 at the laying of the foundation of the temple created so much noise that it could be heard 'far away', and at its dedication the note of joy was still present (6:16). Nearly twenty years later a second group of returning exiles arrived under Ezra the priest, and a new wave of revival broke out at a time when the people had begun to intermarry with the local inhabitants. The record of this is clear in Ezra 10:1: 'While Ezra was praying and confessing, weeping and throwing himself down before the house of God, a large crowd of Israelites—men, women and children—gathered round him. They too wept bitterly.' This was followed by a thorough transformation in the heart and life of the people.

Nehemiah arrived in Jerusalem about the year 445 BC and a further wave of revival followed. This time Ezra read the law to the people, and the Levites followed it with a careful explanation of all that had been read (Nehemiah 8:1–8). The result was almost unprecedented. So broken were the people by the word of the law, that Nehemiah urged them to find their comfort and peace in the Lord (v. 10) and the Levites had to calm the people (v. 11).

The early nineteenth-century revivals in Cornwall, England, reported the 'penitential pain' that a strong conviction of sin brought to the experience of many people; this not infrequently lasted for many hours until peace and joy replaced conviction and grief. This is precisely what we are reading in the time of Nehemiah, almost half a millennium before Pentecost. When the grief of the returned exiles turned into joy, they celebrated the Feast of Tabernacles in a way that had not been known for a thousand years: 'From the days of Joshua son of Nun until that day, the Israelites had not celebrated it like this. And their joy was very great' (Nehemiah 8:17). The same Holy Spirit who was at work in the time of Joshua was at work in the life of the nation in the time of Nehemiah. Later, at the dedication of the walls of Jerusalem, once more the extravagant joy of the people—men, women and children—could be heard 'far away' (Nehemiah 12:43).

There can be little doubt that the period following the return from exile witnessed a significant spiritual revival among the Jews.

Conclusion

Throughout the Old Testament, revival was the way by which God ensured the spiritual survival of his people. Their spiritual life at times was virtually eclipsed by the paganism around them; revival saved the people's faith from dying out altogether. This cycle of decline and revival throughout the Old Testament is mirrored in the story of the Christian church. We cannot attribute the remarkable events in the Acts of the Apostles to the work of the Holy Spirit whilst disallowing his work in similar events under the old covenant. However, as we noted in the previous chapter, we cannot expect

> Throughout the Old Testament, revival was the way by which God ensured the spiritual survival of his people

anything under the old covenant to be as rich and intense as under the new. Old Testament revivals may be thought of as 'pre-Pentecost pentecosts', in much the same way that we have pre-incarnation appearances of Christ in the Old Testament.

4. Experience of revival in the Old Testament

T he purpose of this chapter is to explore in more detail some of the identification tags—or common factors—of the Old Testament revivals referred to previously. These are the hallmarks that reveal their true authorship.

1. Revival follows a period of spiritual decline

Up to the time when 'men began to call on the name of the Lord' (Genesis 4:26) there had been a steady decline from the Fall. The global Flood recorded in Genesis 6 to 8 reveals how widespread the evil was even after the spiritual revival among a part of the human race. Whatever significance we read from Genesis 4:26, it is plain that there had been a long time when people were not calling upon the name of the Lord. If suddenly, out of a dark period of spiritual and moral decay, some begin to call upon the name of the true God, then it is hard to know how else we can describe it other than by the word 'revival'. It may have been this revival in the time of Seth that held back the anger of God and delayed the Flood. Noah was a direct descendant of that godly line of Seth.

At the time of the Exodus from Egypt, the Hebrews had all but forgotten their patriarchal history and God's covenant with them. Even if they were still using the name of the LORD in their worship, it is clear that they did not appreciate its significance. Exodus 6:3 cannot mean that the title was entirely unknown to them since it appears to have been known in the time of Seth (Genesis 4:26) and Abraham was familiar with it (Genesis 15:2). What God was now about to do was to invest the word LORD (YHWH) with a deeper significance than they had ever known. Sinai was a revival of what had been slowly suffocating during the slavery in Egypt. The people's spiritual life was at a desperately low ebb when they cried to God.

From the high point of Sinai there followed forty years of decline that brought a new generation into the promised land. The initial spiritual life of the generation of the conquest slowly deteriorated, until the ominous comment in Judges 2:7 that 'The people served the LORD all the days of Joshua, and all the days of the elders who outlived Joshua'—but not beyond!

The conquest of Canaan was followed by what we know as the period of the judges. This was the darkest time in the history of Israel and the two brightest lights were Deborah (Judges 4–5) and Jephthah (Judges 11–12), both of whom followed periods of spiritual apostasy. Similarly, Samuel began to preach effectively at a time when the light had been extinguished in Israel and this is witnessed by the daughter-in-law of the old priest Eli who named her first born son *Ichabod*, meaning 'no glory'. The loss of the ark of the covenant to the Philistines was symbolic of the departure of the presence of God.

The absence of any account of a specific national revival during the reigns of David and Solomon may prove the very point that we are making. Two kings who were generally godly and wise set the spiritual tone of the nation and there was therefore no need for revival. Revival generally comes after a period of decline, rather than a time of strong spiritual life. Perhaps 1 Kings 8:66 provides us not only with a reflection on the response of the people at the dedication of the temple by Solomon, but with a cameo of their general spiritual well-being throughout the combined eighty years of David and Solomon's reign:

'They blessed the king, and went to their tents joyful and glad of heart for all the good that the Lord had done for his servant David, and for Israel his people.'

During almost three hundred and fifty years of the divided monarchy only three kings experienced revival: Asa, Jehoshaphat and Hezekiah.

They each illustrate revival following a period of decline. Asa's father Abijah was a man who 'committed all the sins his father had done before him' (1 Kings 15:3). And sins they certainly were, including male cult prostitutes, and 'all the idols that his fathers had made' as well as the 'obscene image of Asherah' that his grandmother worshipped (1 Kings 15:12, 13). Only a spiritual awakening could rescue the nation. Sadly, Asa's latter years were not so glorious as his former years, and when his son Jehoshaphat succeeded him, new light was needed in the land.

It was almost ninety years before Judah experienced another spiritual awakening following sixteen years of ungodly rule by Ahaz, the father of Hezekiah. Of Ahaz Scripture comments,

'He walked in the ways of the kings of Israel and also made cast idols for worshipping the Baals. He burned sacrifices in the Valley of Ben-Hinnom and sacrificed his sons in the fire, following the detestable ways of the nations that the Lord had driven out before the Israelites. He offered sacrifices and burned incense at the high places, on the hilltops and under every spreading tree' (2 Chronicles 28:2–4).

Here is a picture of gross immorality and pagan darkness. Many of Hezekiah's own brothers had been sacrificed by fire to the god Ben-Hinnom. Out of this background came Hezekiah and revival.

When the northern kingdom of Israel was conquered by Assyria in 722 BC and Judah was defeated by Babylon in 587 BC, the people were scattered across their known world. Leaderless and dispirited, many of them began to absorb the pagan religions around them and they brought the local gods into their belief alongside the LORD. Young men like Daniel and his friends, who were determined to remain faithful to the God of Israel, could expect little by way of example from those who had been their mentors in Jerusalem (2 Chronicles 36:14). During that period of exile some remained faithful, but many scattered their religion on the ashes of the pagan funeral pyre. In 539 BC God changed the world government and Cyrus, king of the Medo-Persian Empire, allowed the Jews to return home. Out of the darkness of the exile, waves of revival are recorded in the books of Ezra and Nehemiah. The dark days of exile were over.

Whenever the people in the Old Testament experienced revival, it was because they had been walking in darkness for a long time. Significantly, it was during the reign of Hezekiah's godless father, Ahaz, that the prophet Isaiah offered the nation its greatest hope with the promise that 'The people who walked in darkness have seen a great light; those who dwelt in the land of the shadow of death, upon them a light has shined' (Isaiah 9:2). Whilst undoubtedly pointing on to the coming of Messiah, the light of the whole world (vv. 6–7), this promise nevertheless had a partial fulfilment during the reign of Ahaz's godly son Hezekiah.

2. Revival is accompanied by a desperate longing for God

We cannot be sure what '[calling] on the name of the LORD' means in Genesis 4:26, however, given the spiritual and moral state that brought the Flood upon the world in Genesis 6–8, it is not hard to imagine the content of Seth's prayer. Similarly, the groaning and crying out for help by the Israelites in their Egyptian slavery (Exodus 2:23) was an urgent appeal which God answered with a spiritual revival that brought the Hebrews into a national identity that has continued to the present time. Sinai was the beginning of national Israel, which means that Israel as a nation was conceived in the womb of spiritual revival.

Prior to the call of Jephthah to be the ninth judge in Israel, the Spirit of God was stirring the people in an agony of repentance: 'Then the Israelites cried out to the LORD, "We have sinned against you, forsaking our God and serving the Baals … We have sinned. Do with us whatever you think best, but please rescue us now." Then they got rid of the foreign gods among them and served the LORD. And he could bear Israel's misery no longer' (Judges 10:10, 15–16). That was an indispensable precondition for God to visit his people with revival.

During the early ministry of Samuel, we read, 'It was a long time, twenty years in all, that the ark remained at Kiriath Jearim, and all the people of Israel mourned and sought after the LORD' (1 Samuel 7:2). Samuel responded, 'If you are returning to the LORD with all your hearts, then rid yourselves of the foreign gods and the Ashtoreths, and commit yourselves to the LORD, and serve him only…' (1 Samuel 7:3–4).

The same pattern can be found in the times of Asa, Jehoshaphat and Hezekiah. In the time of Asa: 'They entered into a covenant to seek the LORD the God of their fathers with all their heart and soul' (2 Chronicles 15:12). Once he had confessed the sins of the nation, Hezekiah plainly stated his own commitment: 'Now it is in my heart to make a covenant with the LORD God of Israel, that his fierce wrath may turn away from us' (2 Chronicles 29:10). One hundred and forty years after Hezekiah's prayer, Daniel, from his land of exile, was pleading with God for the nation. One of the greatest prayers in the Bible is recorded in Daniel 9. There is an urgency and a desperate longing in Daniel's intercession, which concludes:

'Now, our God, hear the prayers and petitions of your servant. For your sake, O Lord, look with favour on your desolate sanctuary. Give ear, O God, and hear; open your eyes and see the desolation of the city that bears your name. We do not make requests of you because we are righteous, but because of your great mercy. O Lord, listen! O Lord, forgive! O Lord, hear and act! For your sake, O my God, do not delay, because your city and your people bear your name' (Daniel 9:17–19).

Revival came first during the time of Ezra and later through Nehemiah. Psalm 137 is yet another example of the kind of praying that led to the return from exile and the revival that followed. Accompanying revival or preceding it, there is always this heart cry and longing for God to act.

3. God uses leaders in revival

Although God invariably uses leaders in times of revival, they find themselves at the head of a popular movement. Reformation can be imposed, but a mark of revival is a willing and enthusiastic response by the people. We may recall the leaders who were chosen by God: Seth, Moses, Deborah, Jephthah, Samuel, Asa, Jehoshaphat, Hezekiah, Ezra, Nehemiah, Daniel and Ezekiel.

They were leaders of personal courage who were prepared to stand alone if necessary, until the people caught up with them. Moses stood alone on the side of God. Deborah, the prophetess in Judges, gave orders to a king. Samuel showed incredible courage over many years as a lone voice for holiness in a godless land. Asa ousted his grandmother, the Queen Mother, because of her paganism. Jehoshaphat asked for God's advice instead of consulting the false prophets. Hezekiah changed years of ingrained practices that his father had built up. Daniel risked the wrath of five or six pagan despots, and the jaws of lions, in order to take his stand for God. Nehemiah never flinched in the face of enemies who used swords, conspiracies and a fifth column in their attempt to topple him from power. He personally ejected Tobiah from the temple and warned what he would do with the Jewish and foreign traders if they re-opened the market on the sabbath. Nehemiah was a man of uncompromising courage.

They were also men and women with a deep appreciation of the spiritual significance of history. That is an important point. These leaders often recited the history of the nation to spur the people on to action: Moses in Deuteronomy 29:2–18, Jephthah in Judges 11:14–27, Samuel in 1 Samuel 12:6–11, Hezekiah in 2 Chronicles 29:5–11, Daniel in Daniel 9:4–19 and Nehemiah in Nehemiah 9:1–38. They rehearsed the stories of God's past faithfulness and the nation's disobedience. They had an appreciation of the importance and significance of their spiritual history. Those whom God has used in revival ever since, have been encouraged by the knowledge of what God has done in the records of his dealings with his people. See Psalms 44:1; 78:3.

They were also leaders who were thoroughly committed to God's word, to prayer and to personal integrity. The *curriculum vitae* of each of these leaders is in the Bible. Samuel speaks for them all: 'Here I stand. Testify against me in the presence of the LORD and before his anointed. Whose ox have I taken? Whose donkey have I taken? Whom have I cheated? Whom have I oppressed? From whose hand have I accepted a bribe to make me shut my eyes?' (1 Samuel 12:3). Daniel stands as a man against whom even the revealing honesty of the Bible can find no fault and whose character was confirmed by a godless world (Daniel 6:4). None of the Bible leaders was without sin, but all of them were leaders of integrity whose lives were, in general, a model for the nation.

4. Revival always continues as a people's movement

In every instance, revival became a people's movement. After the second giving of the law, Moses reminded the people of their response at Sinai which was 'We will listen and obey', and he reminded them also of the Lord's response:

'I have heard the voice of the words of this people which they have spoken to you. They are right in all that they have spoken. Oh, that they had such a heart in them that they would fear me and always keep all my commandments, that it might be well with them and with their children for ever!' (Deuteronomy 5:28–29).

Whatever actions they may have taken subsequently, and God hints at future failure, the whole congregation of Israel was serious in wanting to follow God. They had every intention of obedience.

After twenty years of faithful preaching, Samuel saw that the people were ready to respond: 'So the children of Israel put away the Baals and the Ashtoreths, and served the LORD only' (1 Samuel 7:3–4). The same was true in the time of Asa: 'They entered into a covenant to seek the LORD God of their fathers with all their heart and soul … They sought God eagerly, and he was found by them' (2 Chronicles 15:12, 15). In the days of Jehoshaphat: 'The people of Judah came together to seek help from the LORD (2 Chronicles 20:4). In the time of Hezekiah: 'The whole assembly bowed in worship … And all whose hearts were willing brought burnt offerings ' (2 Chronicles 29:28, 31).

After the return from exile, in the time of Ezra, 'A large crowd of Israelites—men, women and children—gathered round him. They too wept bitterly … The whole assembly responded with a loud voice, "you are right! We must do as you say"' (Ezra 10:1,12). We read the same response from the people in Nehemiah 8:9–12. When Ezra read the Law of God, 'Then Nehemiah the governor, Ezra the priest and scribe, and the Levites who were instructing the people said to them all, "This day is sacred to the LORD your God. Do not mourn or weep." For all the people had been weeping as they listened to the words of the Law.'

Events even approximating to this today would perhaps convince us that God has visited his people in revival. In each case, revival was a wholehearted, enthusiastic response from the congregation, from a people longing to do what God says.

5. Revival is marked by a careful application of the word of God

The elders of Israel responded to the voice of God from Sinai with a sincere determination to lead the people in whatever way God demanded; they pleaded with Moses: 'Go near and listen to all that the LORD our God says. Then tell us whatever the LORD our God tells you. We will listen and obey' (Deuteronomy 5:27). Even before this, the people's response had been the same, 'The people all responded together, "We will do everything the LORD has said"' (Exodus 19:8).

During the dark period of the judges a knowledge of God's word had not been lost entirely. To the king of Ammon, Jephthah retold the story of Israel at the Exodus and in his account, recorded in Judges 11:17 and 19, Jephthah quoted exactly the words of Numbers 20:17 and 21:22: 'Let us pass through your land.' According to 1 Samuel 3:19 to 4:1, Samuel relayed to the people all that God had revealed to him. Asa and the people determined to seek the Lord, 'and to observe the law and the commandment' (2 Chronicles 14:4). Jehoshaphat's heart was 'devoted to the ways of the LORD', and in the 'evangelism' that followed revival he sent his officials throughout Judah: 'Taking with them the Book of the Law of the LORD; they went round to all the towns of Judah and taught the people' (2 Chronicles 17:9).

The revival in Hezekiah's time was similarly based upon the word of the Lord, and it is noteworthy that the people had 'singleness of heart to obey the command of the king and the leaders, at the word of the LORD' (2 Chronicles 30:12). In addition, prophets were often among the people during these years of the monarchy to give new revelation from God. He sent Azariah in the time of Asa, Jahaziel and Jehu in the reign of Jehoshaphat, and Micah and Isaiah during the revival under Hezekiah.

When the Israelites returned from exile in 539 BC, they returned as a very different people. The nation had lost its city, temple, king and homes. But the people had retained their book. According to Ezra 6:18 everything was done 'as it is written in the Book of Moses'. When they drifted spiritually or morally, the prophets Haggai and Zechariah, and finally Malachi, came to call them back to their biblical moorings. In Nehemiah we have the record of the people—'men and women and all who could hear with understanding'—standing for half a day in the public square in Jerusalem whilst Ezra read from 'the Book of the Law' (Nehemiah 8:2–3). Then the Levites themselves: 'instructed the people in the Law … They read from the Book of the Law of God, making it clear and giving the meaning so that the people could understand what was being read' (Nehemiah 8:8).

6. Revival is accompanied by a conviction of sin and a longing for holiness

When the people of God are confronted by his word accompanied by his Spirit, there is always a longing to be obedient and a hatred of past failure. The elders of Israel insisted that Moses would tell them all that God told him: 'We will hear and do it' (Deuteronomy 5:27). God clearly knew that this represented a genuine desire on their part because his response through Moses was in the form of a wistful desire that they might always think like this: 'Oh, that their hearts would be inclined to fear me and keep all my commands always, so that it might go well with them and their children for ever!' (v. 29).

Prior to the leadership of Jephthah, Israel cried out to God: 'We have sinned against you, because we have both forsaken our God and served the Baals' (Judges 10:10). In fact, their desperate case is revealed by their response when the Lord told them to cry to 'the gods which you have chosen' (v. 14). 'We have sinned,' they repeated. 'Do to us whatever seems best to you' (v. 15)—and they discarded all their false idols.

Hezekiah acknowledged the sins of his fathers as if they were his own (2 Chronicles 29:6–7), and his repentance is seen in the number of burnt offerings that he and the Levites offered following that prayer. In the land of exile Daniel cried, 'We have sinned. We have done wrong.' Ezra was found praying, confessing, weeping and throwing himself down before the house of God, and soon the men, women and children who had gathered 'wept very bitterly' (Ezra 10:1). Later, as the law was read and explained to the people, they wept continually, and Nehemiah and the Levites had to calm the people saying, 'Do not grieve, for the joy of the LORD is your strength...' (Nehemiah 8:10–11).

This 'penitential pain' is found throughout the history of revival.

7. Revival transforms worship

Sinai introduced a new seriousness among the people. They trembled because they feared God. In Deuteronomy 6, for example, the emphasis is upon obedience, fear and righteousness. Almost every verse refers directly or indirectly to one of these three. The early chapters of Deuteronomy are primarily concerned to remind the people of the law, their history and their privileges, and to ensure that their worship remained pure. Commenting on the cruel and vile religious practices of the surrounding tribes, God warned 'You must not worship the LORD your God in their way ... be careful not to be ensnared by enquiring about their gods' (Deuteronomy 12:4, 8, 30).

Moses had inherited a rag-tag of runaway slaves. They had little true religion and therefore no true worship; they had no acknowledged leadership and no defined laws; they counted for nothing and were 'the fewest of all peoples' (Deuteronomy 7:7). Fifty years later Moses left them as a nation with organized leadership, clear laws for life, a firm understanding of the character of the true God, a knowledge of how to worship in fear and purity, and an eagerness to be obedient to the Lord. All this was achieved not merely by the rule of law and the charismatic leadership of Moses, but by the Spirit of God who, though infrequently mentioned in the records, was clearly at work among the people.

Whenever the nation experienced new life towards God, their worship changed. Asa 'removed the foreign altars and the high places, smashed the sacred stones and cut down the Asherah poles' (2 Chronicles 14:2–3). Jehoshaphat 'removed the high places and the Asherah poles from Judah' (2 Chronicles 17:6). In the first month of his reign Hezekiah reopened the doors of the temple and re-established true worship (2 Chronicles 29:3,5).

The psalmist once pleaded for revival so that 'your people may rejoice in you' (Psalm 85:6). When the people became serious about God, they approached him not only with awesome fear but with great joy. Fear and joy are twins in true worship.

Under Asa 'all Judah rejoiced about the oath because they had sworn it wholeheartedly. They sought God eagerly, and he was found by them' (2 Chronicles 15:15). In the time of Hezekiah: 'Hezekiah and all the people rejoiced at what God had brought about for his people, because it was done so quickly (2 Chronicles 29:36) and the Levites 'sang praises with gladness' (v. 30). 'They celebrated joyfully ... [and] the entire assembly of Judah rejoiced ... There was great joy in Jerusalem' (2 Chronicles 30:23–26). It was described as exceeding anything that had happened since the time of Solomon (v 26).

In the time of Nehemiah, he encouraged the people to move on from their sorrow over sin: 'Go and enjoy choice food and sweet drinks, and send some to those who have nothing prepared. This day is sacred to our Lord. Do not grieve, for the joy of the LORD is your strength.' The Levites calmed the people: 'Be still, for this is a sacred day. Do not grieve.' Then 'all the people went away to eat and drink, to send portions of food and to celebrate with great joy, because they now understood the words that had been made known to them.' The people celebrated 'with great joy' (Nehemiah 8:10–12). There is an interesting retrospective comment in Nehemiah 8:17: the worship of the returning exiles is described as without precedent: 'From the days of Joshua son of Nun until that day, the Israelites had not celebrated it like this. And their joy was very great.'

8. Revival is evident to the surrounding neighbourhood

Revival knows no hiding place and no disguise. The world around knows what God is doing. This was the basis of Moses' plea to God in Exodus 33:16: 'How will anyone know that you are pleased with me and with your people unless you go with us? What else will distinguish me and your people from all the other people on the

> Revival knows no hiding place and no disguise. The world around knows what God is doing

face of the earth?' Moses knew that the spiritual health of the nation was vital for its testimony to the surrounding tribes. When Moses prayed, 'If your Presence does not go with us, do not send us up from here' (v. 15), he was pleading for the presence of God to be revealed in a remarkable way. It was not only the dramatic events of the crossing of the Red Sea that caused the nations to fear (Exodus 15:16), but the quality life and evident blessing on God's people had the same effect: 'All the peoples on earth will see that you are called by the name of the LORD, and they will fear you' (Deuteronomy 28:10).

When Asa assembled the tribes of Judah and Benjamin, he discovered that 'large numbers had come over to him from Israel when they saw that the Lord his God was with him' (2 Chronicles 15:9). He called together the tribes of Judah and Benjamin and when he counted them, he discovered there were more than there should be; others had drifted down from Israel! This was incredible because the north and south had been bitter enemies for generations.

Even more unusual was the fact that during the reign of Jehoshaphat the surrounding nations brought gifts and tributes to the king who had not defeated them militarily:

'The fear of the LORD fell on all the kingdoms of the lands surrounding Judah, so that they did not make war with Jehoshaphat. Some Philistines brought Jehoshaphat gifts and silver as tribute, and the Arabs brought him flocks' (2 Chronicles 17:10–11).

The only other time such things occurred was during the reign of Solomon. On that occasion the nations were impressed by the king's renowned wisdom (1 Kings 4:34).

These were times of direct evangelism as well. Jehoshaphat went up and down the land from Beersheba to Ephraim and brought the people 'back to the Lord God of their fathers' (2 Chronicles 19:4). Similarly, Hezekiah sent out couriers throughout all Israel and Judah to invite the people to return to the lord (2 Chronicles 30:1–10). Nations and neighbours knew what was happening in Jerusalem.

9. Revival rarely lasts beyond one generation

The generation that was revived at the Exodus died in the wilderness because of their subsequent disobedience, and a new generation had to seek God for itself. The generation under Joshua remained faithful but another grew up who 'did not know the LORD nor the work which he had done for Israel' (Judges 2:10). These people ushered in the dark period of the judges. Nothing followed the leadership of Deborah, or Jephthah, except more darkness. The same generation that responded to the preaching of Samuel was soon demanding a king and rejecting God as their leader. Hezekiah stands between a godless father, Ahaz, and an even more godless son, Manasseh.

The fact that Jehoshaphat followed Asa is possibly unique in Old Testament narrative, and there is a significant note in 2 Chronicles 17:3 that the Lord was with Jehoshaphat because 'in his early years he walked in the ways that his father David had followed.' The tragedy of those three great kings is that each—Asa, Jehoshaphat and Hezekiah—were less faithful towards the end of their lives. Revival can end by the hand of those through whom it began. After the heady days of Ezra and Nehemiah there followed four hundred years of spiritual wilderness for Israel.

It is instructive to study how revival ends and not just how it begins. God often allows the frailty of men to destroy his work. The sinful failure of leaders can end a revival, and sometimes revival is organized out of existence by the church. At other times, however, God simply withdraws his hand. Whatever the cause, each generation must seek God for itself. God will not allow us to trade on the spiritual capital of our fathers.

> God will not allow us to trade on the spiritual capital of our fathers

5. Expectation of revival in the Old Testament

In chapter 7 we will look at the varied views of end times as they relate to revival. It is sufficient here to comment in brief. For those who believe that Christ will come and establish his personal and earthly rule in Jerusalem for one thousand years (premillennialism), we may read all Old Testament prophecies of revival to refer to this period. Those who believe that before Christ returns there will be a golden age of gospel success (postmillennialism), the same passages may be seen as a promise of the revivals that must come in order to arrive at that final 'golden age'. If we understand the one thousand years of Revelation 20:3 and 7 as a reference to the whole period of the age of the gospel (amillennialism) we may assume that all Old Testament prophecies of revival refer to this period also. There is even an 'optimistic amillennialism' that confidently hopes for revival, and a 'pessimistic amillennialism' that believes the day of grace has passed. Our view of the millennium may significantly govern whether or not we expect regular revivals in the history of the church.

However, for this chapter it will be assumed that all passages that imply an expectation of revival are just that—whenever it may happen.

Although it is generally a sound principle to interpret the Old Testament in the light of the New, the wide divergence of views in interpreting Revelation 20 may point to the fact that, in this case, we may be wiser to work in the opposite direction. If we start with the Old Testament, we will find that throughout that period there was an expectation of periodic times of spiritual revival. We can see this as an expectation for *immediate* revival, *intermediate* revival, and *ultimate* revival.

The Old Testament expectation of immediate revival

Moses spoke confidently to the Israelites of revival shortly before his death. He reminded the people of God's covenant of holiness and warned that disobedience would bring severe judgement from God and disgrace in the eyes of the nations (Deuteronomy 29:24–28). However, in Deuteronomy 30:1–10 we have a description of what God will do when 'you and your children return to the LORD your God and obey him with all your heart and with all your soul according to everything I command you today…' Moses promised not only national blessing, but much more: 'The LORD your God will circumcise your hearts and the hearts of your descendants, so that you may love him with all your heart and with all your soul, and live' (v. 6). In the light of Paul's claim that 'circumcision is circumcision of the heart, by the Spirit, not by the written code' (Romans 2:29), Moses' promise 'God will circumcise your hearts' is an old covenant description of revival.

God offered his people a simple choice: at all times throughout their history they could choose death and destruction through disobedience, or life and prosperity through obedience. If they first made the wrong choice, at any time they could move from the bad to the good through spiritual revival which would be God's response to true repentance. The promise in Deuteronomy 30:6 was vital for the future life of Israel and it was never forgotten.

In Psalm 138:7 David reflects on Deuteronomy 30 by using a word that has as its root the same word Moses used when he encouraged the people to choose life. David said, 'Though I walk in the midst of trouble, you preserve my life.' A better translation would be 'you will revive me' because the word means 'to quicken' or 'give life'. David knew about the promise in Deuteronomy 30 and he used it in his time of need. The same word is used in Psalm 85:6: 'Will you not revive us again, that your people may rejoice in you?' In Psalm 77 Asaph based his hope for future rescue by God upon his knowledge of what God had done in the past, and his closing reference is to the leading of God in the time of Moses and Aaron.

This concept of revival is based upon the transition from the bad to the good, from the barren to the spiritually fruitful, and it was something that was well known in the Old Testament. Jehoshaphat seems to have had this promise in mind when he pleaded with God in the words recorded in 2 Chronicles 20:9, 'If calamity comes upon us … we will stand in your presence before this temple that bears your Name and will cry out to you in our distress, and you will hear us and save us.' Notice the certainty, 'we will' and 'you will'. Such confidence can only stem from reliance upon a firm promise from God.

At the end of the history of the Old Testament, Ezra the priest turned to the same word 'revive' when he gave thanks to God for the new spiritual life God had given to his people at the return from exile:

'Now for a brief moment favour has been shown by the LORD our God, to leave us a remnant and to give us a secure hold within his holy place, that our God may brighten our eyes and grant us a little *reviving* in our slavery. For we are slaves. Yet our God has not forsaken us in our slavery, but has extended to us his steadfast love before the kings of Persia, to grant us some *reviving*, to set up the house of our God, to repair its ruins, and to give us protection in Judea and Jerusalem' (Ezra 9:8–9 ESV 2001).

The same Hebrew word is used in each instance where the word 'reviving' occurs. The strength of this word is seen by its use in 1 Kings 17:22 where the Lord restored to life the widow's son in response to Elijah's prayer 'and the life of the child came into him again, and he *revived*.'

In Psalm 80:3, 7, 19, the psalmist prays three times, 'Restore us, O God.' Although a different word is used, it is one that basically means 'to return'. Similarly, in Psalm 85:4 the prayer is 'Restore us again, O God of our salvation.' The whole of this psalm clearly expresses a belief that there is a case to plead with God and the psalmist expects a response. Restoring and reviving are synonymous terms here. Psalm 126 is a psalm of praise for the return from captivity and that great event is seen as a time of spiritual restoration and revival.

The same expectation is found in some of the public prayers of the kings in the Old Testament. This promise of Deuteronomy 30:2–6 is the basis of Solomon's prayer at the dedication of the temple recorded in 1 Kings 8:46–53. It was a prayer based firmly on what God had spoken 'by your servant Moses' (v. 53). Solomon's prayer, 'May he turn our hearts to him to walk in all his ways and to keep the commands, decrees and regulations he gave our fathers' (1 Kings 8:58) must be a reflection of Moses' assurance, 'The LORD your God will circumcise your hearts and the hearts of your descendants, so that you may love him with all your heart and with all your soul, and live' (Deuteronomy 30:6).

Even when Isaiah is prophesying in the full hope of the Messianic age, he cannot stop himself from entering an urgent plea for immediate revival based upon the known character of God: 'Oh, that you would rend the heavens and come down, that the mountains would tremble before you! As when fire sets twigs ablaze and causes water to boil, come down to make your name known to your enemies and cause the nations to quake before you!' (Isaiah 64:1–2). The often-quoted chapter of Isaiah 35 must refer, at least in the first instance, to the revival that is recorded in 2 Chronicles 29 in the time of Hezekiah, king of Judah.

An even closer link with Deuteronomy 30 is found when Jeremiah wrote a letter to the Jews in exile, eight hundred years after Moses. His prophecy recorded in Jeremiah 29 contains the phrase: 'I will bring you back from captivity' (v. 14). This is the same expression as that found in Deuteronomy 30:3. Most likely Jeremiah had the promise of Moses in mind. King Jehoshaphat appears to have taken up the same promise when he affirms, 'If calamity comes upon us ... we will cry out to you in our distress, and you will hear and save' (2 Chronicles 20:9).There is no uncertainty here because the king had just reminded God of his care over his people in the time of Moses (v. 7) and this in turn reminded the king of the promise given through that great leader. Jehoshaphat was confident of restoration because of the promise.

Similarly, the prophet Joel appears to have Deuteronomy 30:2 in mind: 'When you and your children return to the LORD your God and obey him with all your heart and with all your soul…'. In Joel 2:12–17 the nation is encouraged to return to the Lord on the basis of his known character of compassion and mercy; they should 'gather the people, sanctify the congregation, assemble the elders, gather the children and nursing babes…' and plead with the Lord to spare his people. There are unmistakable reflections of Deuteronomy 30 here. This is precisely what God had encouraged his people to do whenever they were in trouble. Joel 2:19, 23–24 is the exact fulfilment of God's promised blessing for a people who return to him in repentance.

With the benefit of our knowledge of Acts 2:16–21 we may understand the fuller significance of Joel's prophecy, but it is not likely that the Old Testament prophet, reviewing the course of Israel's history up to his day in the seventh century BC, knew that the nation had more than half a millennium to wait for the great revival of Pentecost. Without doubt the judgements of Joel 3:1–16 and 19–21 were anticipated by the people in Joel's own day and the material (or spiritual?) blessings colourfully described in vv. 17–18 would follow. It is reasonable to assume that in the prophet's mind, and that of his hearers, the personal and national revival of 2:28–32 would also be immediate.

Daniel, in his prayer from the land of exile, went back in his mind to the curses and blessings of Moses: 'Just as it is written in the Law of Moses, all this disaster has come upon us, yet we have not sought the favour of the LORD our God by turning from our sins and giving attention to your truth' (Daniel 9:13). Then at the end of his prayer we have one of the strongest demands ever made upon God in the Old Testament record. Daniel looked for a reviving, and confidently expected it on the ground of God's covenant promises through Moses recorded in Deuteronomy 30:

'Now, our God, hear the prayers and petitions of your servant. For your sake, O LORD, look with favour on your desolate sanctuary. Give ear, O God, and hear; open your eyes and see the desolation of the city that bears your Name. We do not make requests of you because we are righteous, but because of your great mercy. O LORD, listen! O LORD, forgive! O LORD, hear and act! For your sake, O my God, do not delay, because your city and your people bear your Name.' (Daniel 9:17–19).

Ezekiel undoubtedly expected much more for the exiles than simply a return to the city of Jerusalem. In Ezekiel 37:14 he promised them on behalf of God: 'I will put my Spirit in you and you will live, and I will settle you in your own land. Then you will know that I the LORD have spoken, and I have done it, declares the LORD.' That this whole prophecy refers to the return from exile in the typically vivid language of the prophets (v. 12 for example), is undoubted. But it has a reference to much more than simply the nation returning to its homeland. The reference to the Spirit must refer to a spiritual revival. This is underlined by the extravagant promise of 39:29: '"I will no longer hide my face from them, for I will pour out my Spirit on the house of Israel", declares the Sovereign LORD.'

The ultimate fulfilment of Ezekiel's promise is at Pentecost, especially because of the similarity to Joel 2:28–29, but the whole context of the Ezekiel passage is the return from captivity. Our best understanding is to see the events recorded in Ezra and Nehemiah as a fulfilment of this promise and an example of Old Testament revival; what we have previously referred to as a pre-Pentecost pentecost.

One thing appears certain in all these examples: whether it was David, Solomon, Jehoshaphat, Isaiah, Daniel or Ezekiel, they all longed for and expected revival in their own time. The possibility of it was a living reality with them. They knew that if the people repented and turned to God, at any time he might turn to them and revive them again because it was the nature of his promises and character to do so.

We must not flatten this expectation by adding a timescale to the prophecies in the light of what we know with the benefit of the whole story of the Bible. Sometimes we know when a particular prophecy was fulfilled, but the prophets and the people did not always have our advantage. When the prophet Joel promised the beleaguered people of Judah with his extravagant prophecy of the Holy Spirit, it would hardly have encouraged them if he had added: 'This will happen approximately eight hundred years from now.' Similarly, it is no criticism of Paul in the New Testament when he wrote as if the Second Coming of Christ would be very soon. It was no business of his to know when, but only to ensure that the people lived in constant expectation of its any-time reality. It would not have been much comfort to the first-century Christians in persecution to hear, 'Be encouraged, in two thousand years or more Jesus will return.'

The Old Testament expectation of intermediate revival

There were times when a prophet knew that the fulfilment of his words lay further in the future. Occasionally they were given precise time-scales in advance. From reading Jeremiah, Daniel knew exactly when the exile would draw to a close (Jeremiah 29:10–14 and compare Daniel 9:2).

Isaiah 35 is an encouraging picture of God reviving and restoring his people. The question presents itself: when is this going to happen? Most Bible commentators appear to know the answer, although it is doubtful whether Isaiah did. Some suggest that this chapter is a picture of the one thousand years earthly rule of Christ; others claim it is a beautiful description of the church under general revival; whilst others see it as a picture of the age in which we are now living or a description of the final new heavens and new earth.

One thing is beyond doubt: nothing like Isaiah 35 happened in the time of Isaiah, nor even during the reign of Hezekiah. Perhaps it has a partial fulfilment at the return from exile in 538 BC—one hundred and fifty years later. Isaiah was therefore looking at least for an intermediate fulfilment; he may not have expected it to happen in his own time, but it was coming and would appear not long after his death.

Two more passages in Isaiah clearly expect revival and it will be helpful to use them as examples of how we should apply Old Testament prophecy—not according to our preconceived plan, but according to the natural meaning of the passages themselves. The first is in chapter 41:17–20:

'The poor and needy search for water, but there is none; their tongues are parched with thirst. But I the LORD will answer them; I, the God of Israel, will not forsake them. I will make rivers flow on barren heights, and springs within the valleys. I will turn the desert into pools of water, and the parched ground into springs. I will put in the desert the cedar and the acacia, the myrtle and the olive. I will set pines in the wasteland, the fir and the cypress together, so that people may see and know, may consider and understand, that the hand of the LORD has done this, that the Holy One of Israel has created it.'

The other passage in Isaiah is found in chapter 44:1–5:

'But now listen, O Jacob, my servant, Israel, whom I have chosen. This is what the LORD says—he who made you, who formed you in the womb, and who will help you: Do not be afraid, O Jacob, my servant, Jeshurun, whom I have chosen. For I will pour water on the thirsty land, and streams on the dry ground; I will pour out my Spirit on your offspring, and my blessing on your descendants. They will spring up like grass in a meadow, like poplar trees by flowing streams. One will say, 'I belong to the LORD'; another will call himself by the name of Jacob; still another will write on his hand, 'The LORD's', and will take the name Israel.'

Isaiah 40 refers to the coming of the Messiah because it is the prophetic chapter pointing on to John the Baptist: 'A voice of one calling in the desert, prepare the way of the Lord, make straight in the wilderness a highway for our God' (v. 3). That much is clear. What is even more significant for our purpose is the fact that Cyrus, king of the Medo-Persian Empire, is mentioned by name (44:28 and 45:1, 13) as the destroyer of Babylon and rebuilder of Jerusalem. Since this is a despot who rose to power one hundred and fifty years beyond Isaiah, the reference has provided a field-day for the scepticism of Bible critics. However, it proves only that God can be specific when he wishes to be (compare 1 Kings 13:2). For our interest is the fact that the introduction of the name of a king not yet born, together with a prophecy for 'your offspring, and … your descendants' (Isaiah 44:3) makes it certain that Isaiah knew that this promise was not likely to be fulfilled within his own lifetime. It would have an 'intermediate fulfilment'.

Alec Motyer is correct when he writes of Isaiah's prophecies: 'The whole book is a huge mosaic' in which prophecies that are intended for the immediate future are made to serve for any time. Motyer continues that Isaiah does not offer a time-scale for the fulfilment of his prophecies.[35]

The passages from Isaiah 41 and 44 that speak of revival, come between Isaiah 40 and 45. But what do chapters 40 and 45 refer to—the time of the Messiah or the time of Cyrus? There is very little doubt for us. So much of chapters 40–44 are used in the New Testament and applied to Christ (for Isaiah 40:3 see Matthew 3:3; for Isaiah 40:4 see Luke 3:5; for Isaiah 42:1–3 see Matthew 12:18–20; and for Isaiah 42:7 see Luke 1:79). The reference must be to the coming Messiah. Chapter 45 opens a new prophecy specifically relating to Cyrus. For Isaiah both the time of the Messiah and the time of Cyrus are periods of glorious revival. He did not know when they would come, but that they *would* come was not in doubt. Isaiah is therefore looking forward to intermediate revival, not ultimate

---

35 Alec Motyer, *The Prophecy of Isaiah* (IVP, 1993), pp. 29, 31–32.

revival; he was looking forward to revival both in the days of Cyrus, king of Persia and, though he probably was not aware of the full significance of his words, in the time of the Messiah also.

The prophet Amos provides us with a further example of this. Chapter 9:11–15 is clearly about a time of spiritual revival:

'"In that day I will restore David's fallen tent. I will repair its broken places, restore its ruins, and build it as it used to be, so that they may possess the remnant of Edom and all the nations that bear my name," declares the LORD, who will do these things. "The days are coming," declares the LORD, "when the reaper will be overtaken by the ploughman and the planter by the one treading grapes. New wine will drip from the mountains and flow from all the hills. I will bring back my exiled people Israel; they will rebuild the ruined cities and live in them. They will plant vineyards and drink their wine; they will make gardens and eat their fruit. I will plant Israel in their own land, never again to be uprooted from the land I have given them", says the LORD your God'.

When will this be? It may be at the return from exile under Cyrus, which was two hundred years ahead of Amos. Some claim that because the passage refers to rebuilding the city it is a picture of the earthly reign of Christ over Jerusalem. Others will suggest that it is a picture of the golden age of the gospel prior to the return of Christ. But we are not really left in any doubt what it refers to. At the Council of Jerusalem in Acts 15, James quoted from Amos 9:11–12 and concluded that its ultimate fulfilment had been when the gospel of Jesus Christ was preached among the Gentiles (Acts 15:12–18). The Scripture is its own interpreter here, and we must work from the Bible and not from our pre-planned scheme. James in effect says, 'This is that'. Just as Peter on the day of Pentecost had said the same of Joel 2.

Amos is therefore looking for intermediate revival beyond his own day but before the final end; although, again, the timing may have been beyond the knowledge of the prophet. It is in fact common among the prophets for them to give a prophecy that has an intermediate fulfilment (beyond their own time, yet before the Messiah comes) and a more distant fulfilment. Jeremiah gives us an example of precisely this when he is promising the return from exile and at one point 'overshoots' with, what would at that time have been, the mysterious reference to Rachel weeping in Ramah (Jeremiah 31:15; compare Matthew 2:8).

The Old Testament prophets believed therefore in a God of immediate any-time revival, and of intermediate future-time revival. Unknown to them, the intermediate revival could be either at the return from exile in 539 BC or beyond this into the Messianic age—or both.

The Old Testament expectation of ultimate revival

Will there be revival right at the end, before the end of this age? Isaiah 34 and 35 provide us with typical examples of scriptures used by those looking for an end-time revival. Even if chapter 35 has a partial fulfilment in the time of Hezekiah or at the return from exile under Cyrus, the language is far too rich and extravagant to be limited to those periods alone.

The sixteenth century Reformer John Calvin has no doubt as to its ultimate fulfilment when he comments on Isaiah 35:

'The Lord began some kind of restoration when he brought his people out of Babylon; but that was only a slight foretaste, and, therefore I have no hesitation in saying that this passage, as well as others of a similar kind, must refer to the kingdom of Christ ... By the kingdom of Christ I mean not only that which is begun here, but that which shall be completed at the last day ... Because believers will never find perfect rest till that day arrives. And the reason why the prophets speak of the kingdom of Christ in such lofty terms is, that they look at that end when the true happiness of believers shall be most fully restored.'

Calvin therefore understood Isaiah 35 as a picture of a partial fulfilment in the time of Hezekiah or an intermediate fulfilment in the time of

Cyrus and the return from exile, but more significantly the blessing of Christ through the gospel received now, and also as a picture of the final kingdom of Christ at the close of this age.[36] For Calvin therefore, Isaiah 35 is immediate, intermediate and ultimate in its fulfilment—for him, the ultimate is heaven.

A more extended illustration of this is found in Isaiah 60 to 65. Isaiah 60 clearly refers to the gospel age and chapter 61 describes the work of Christ. It opens with the words, 'The Spirit of the LORD God is upon me, because the LORD has anointed me to preach good tidings to the poor; he has sent me to heal the broken-hearted, to proclaim liberty to the captives, and the opening of the prison to those who are bound.' Jesus himself read from this passage and announced, 'Today this Scripture is fulfilled in your hearing' (Luke 4:16–21). Isaiah 61 must therefore ultimately refer to the ministry of Christ, and because the previous chapter stands inextricably with it, that too must refer to the gospel age. Here, Isaiah is presenting the benefits of the gospel in pictures belonging to the Old Testament.

Isaiah 62 therefore is not only a heart cry from the prophet, but it is a description of the purpose of the Messiah: he will not be quiet until the righteousness of God's people shines out like the dawn (v. 1). The theme of judgement and salvation follows through chapters 63, 64 and 65 with an intermediate cry for revival in chapter 64:1, 'Oh, that you would rend the heavens! That you would come down! That the mountains might shake at your presence ... [come down] to make your name known to your adversaries, that the nations may tremble at your presence!' At this point Isaiah brings us to a description of what he calls 'new heavens and a new earth' in chapter 65:17–25 which is linked with Revelation 21:1–2. It is quite clear therefore that when Isaiah arrives at chapter 65 he finds himself at the establishment of the kingdom of God—a heavenly kingdom.

---

36 See Calvin's Commentary on Isaiah.

Here then is the pattern: Isaiah introduces the Messiah, quickly scans what we know as the age of the gospel, and then goes straight to the new heavens and the new earth. Isaiah 66 is a final challenge to the Jews of Isaiah's day: in the light of these great promises of the gospel and heaven, the old order has passed away.

Joel follows a similar pattern. He was preaching possibly during the reign of King Joash (if so, about 800 BC) and a summary of chapters 1 and 2 would be 'repent, repent, repent'. In chapter 2:19 the prophet introduces a time of spiritual revival. But the prophecy must be looking beyond the return from exile in 539 BC. In fact, beyond any reference to earthly Israel, because verse 19 has never been fulfilled from that day to this: 'I will no longer make you a reproach among the nations.'

The next section, vv. 20–27, cannot refer to a millennium either before or after the return of Christ, because verse 28 begins a new section with the words 'and afterwards'—and then follows the description of Pentecost. It is another picture of revival, and in Acts 2:17 Peter removes any doubt as to the application of this passage. We can only consistently read Joel 2:18–27 as another occasion where New Testament truths are presented in Old Testament language and the reference must be to the coming of the Messiah.

Joel 2:28–32 is therefore unquestionably a prophecy of the day of Pentecost. In vivid language (vv. 30–31) the unique events of that day are described. How far it can be taken as a description of the whole of the gospel age is a matter of debate, but one thing is certain: the obvious picture language of verses 30–31 should guard us against taking any of the symbols of prophetic language as having a literal fulfilment. Like a piece of music being transposed into a different key, Old Testament prophecy needs to be interpreted into a New Testament fulfilment.

Joel 3:2 takes us right on to the Day of Judgement when he speaks of the Valley of Jehoshaphat. This valley is in the wilderness of Tekoa, south east of Jerusalem, where God destroyed Judah's enemies (2 Chronicles

20); the name means 'The Lord judges'. It was a symbol of God calling the nation to account. Much of Joel 3 is linked with the book of Revelation: Joel 3:13 compare Revelation 14:17–20. Joel 3:16 compare Revelation 21:3. Joel 3:17 compare Revelation 21:27 and 22:3. Joel 3:18 compare Revelation 22:1–2.

Whilst Joel 3:18–21 is a glorious picture of revival, since it follows the terrible day of judgement it must be the ultimate revival of the new Jerusalem when heaven becomes a reality for the people of God. This is like nothing on earth, it is heavenly Jerusalem. Once again spiritual blessings are clothed in Old Testament picture language.

Isaiah 2:2–4 is another example of the gospel presented in Old Testament language:

'In the last days the mountain of the LORD's temple will be established as chief among the mountains; it will be raised above the hills, and all nations will stream to it. Many peoples will come and say, "Come, let us go up to the mountain of the LORD, to the house of the God of Jacob. He will teach us his ways, so that we may walk in his paths." The law will go out from Zion, the word of the LORD from Jerusalem. He will judge between the nations and will settle disputes for many peoples. They will beat their swords into ploughshares and their spears into pruning hooks. Nation will not take up sword against nation, nor will they train for war anymore.'

Peter leaves little doubt as to the correct application of this passage in Isaiah 2. Joel 2:28 begins, 'And it shall come to pass afterward'; in Acts 2:17 Peter chooses to render it 'in the last days'. That phrase 'in the last days' is exactly Isaiah 2:2. Since Joel 2 refers to the gospel era, it is therefore clear that description given of 'the last days' in Isaiah 2:3–4 is also a reference to the benefits of the gospel, and not to any final millennium.

Conclusion

The possibility of immediate any-time revival was always in front of the nation of Israel because of God's promises through Moses recorded particularly in Deuteronomy 30. True repentance could usher in a spiritual revival in the life of the people belonging to God. Many of the prophets also looked confidently to the time of intermediate revival. This would either be at the return from exile, or well beyond their own day. Some looked on to the restoring of the fortunes of Israel during the days of the Messiah and the following gospel age. They could only describe this in their extravagantly pictorial Old Testament language.

At that point the prophets generally stop. They go no further than to begin with Jesus, the Messiah, and give an overview of the gospel age. Sometimes they may be specific, like Joel referring to the day of Pentecost. When they do look beyond the gospel age, the only thing they see is judgement and then the ultimate kingdom of God.

The prophets have nothing else in mind. They offer the Messiah, the gospel age, ultimate judgement and the end. There is no indication of a golden age of spiritual revival and gospel success at the end of this age just before, or just after, the return of Jesus Christ. No millennial hope beyond the glorious age of the Messiah—the age of the gospel. The character of God and the strength of his promises, consistently understood, is where we should establish the ground for our hope.

It is doubtful whether the prophets worked to the same timescale that we can enjoy in retrospect. The concepts of Old Testament and New Testament, before and after Christ, are peculiar to the Christian era. For the saints who lived before the birth of Christ, history was certainly pointing to the coming Messiah, but who can know whether or not Isaiah hoped that he would live to see the fulfilment of his prophecy in 44:1–5?

The prophets certainly expected that, given the true repentance of the nation, God could bring revival at any time; this was always their hope. As we have seen, there is evidence also that they expected intermediate revival beyond their own time and into the gospel age. But they did not make this claim directly, because that was not their brief; their task was to prepare the way for the Messiah and to describe him and his ministry up to the final Judgement.

Because God revealed himself to his prophets in the Old Testament as an any-time reviving God, there is no reason why we should not follow that principle through into the gospel age. If he was a reviving God in the Old Testament, why should he not be the same in the New Testament? Everything God did by his Spirit under the old covenant he does more lavishly by his Spirit under the new. It is consistent with our view of the unchanging character of God that unless he reveals to the contrary, we may assume that the way he acted for his people Israel under the first covenant is the same as his care for his church under the second. It would be remarkably strange that the God who pledged himself to restore the spiritual condition of Israel when they called out of desperation for help, does not offer at least the same hope to the church.

Even if there is no specific golden age of revival on earth prophesied, the experience, examples and expectations of immediate and intermediate revival throughout the Old Testament give us authority to pray for revival at any time. In addition to this, if we find revival spoken of and expected in the New Testament, we can return to the Old Testament and use—with even greater certainty—those passages that long for revival. Our God is unchanging in his grace towards his repentant people. The character of God therefore is our ground for pleading with him to 'turn us again' and 'rend the heavens and come down'. It is our confidence for the bold cry, 'Awake, O LORD!' (Psalm 44:23).

6. Expectation of revival in the New Testament

The New Testament covers only half a century of early church history compared with sixteen hundred years from Abraham to Malachi—and much more before Abraham. However, the God of the New Testament is the God of the Old Testament also. In Old Testament prophecy the coming of Christ and the birth of the Christian church is described as a period of great spiritual revival that was to be magnificently beyond anything known under the old order. We have seen how the prophets used extravagant language, often through the symbol of water, to describe revival.

Some of the traditionally used texts for revival come in that form of imagery. One example is Isaiah 41:18: 'I will make rivers flow on barren heights, and springs within the valleys. I will turn the desert into pools of water, and the parched ground into springs.' Another is Isaiah 44:3–4, 'I will pour water on the thirsty land, and streams on the dry ground; I will pour out my Spirit on your offspring, and my blessing on your descendants. They will spring up like grass in a meadow, like poplar trees by flowing streams.'

Those are two of a number of passages in the Old Testament where the possibility of intermediate revival is spoken of in the vivid imagery of God bringing springs of water on thirsty land.

These prophecies began to be fulfilled when Jesus stood up in the celebration of a great festival in Jerusalem and declared, 'If anyone is thirsty, let him come to me and drink. Whoever believes in me, as the Scripture has said, streams of living water will flow from within him' (John 7:37–38). John commented, 'By this he meant the Spirit, whom those who believed in him were later to receive' (John 7:39). Jesus therefore took up the imagery of passages like Isaiah 41 and 44 and applied it to the outpouring of the Holy Spirit at Pentecost. This is the first confirmation of revival in the gospel age. Although some have made a case for revival as a description of the ministry of both John the Baptist and Jesus when vast crowds followed them and many lives were changed.[37]

However, did the expectation of revival end with the coming of Christ and the day of Pentecost, or was that a new beginning? Is there evidence from the New Testament that the prophets looked forward to more beyond Pentecost? And did the New Testament writers themselves expect something more? Part of our answer will be the conclusion that we have already drawn, namely, that the Old Testament prophets saw God as an any-time reviving God. Consequently, there is no reason why we should not follow that same God into the gospel age. That is an inference drawn from the unchangeable character of God. It is a powerful inference—but there is more that can be said.

The question may be asked: 'Doesn't the New Testament expect Christian communities to go steadily forward and live consistently filled with the Spirit? Revival implies a period of spiritual coldness or backsliding from which we must be restored by the Holy Spirit. Is that a New Testament concept?' Our first answer must be to insist that an Old Testament experience of the church is there for our instruction and it remains relevant for the New Testament church unless it is specifically countermanded in the New or is seen to be no longer appropriate because of New Testament principles. The Acts of the Apostles covers only thirty years of the history of the early church and that may be too short a period to assess the work of the Spirit in the church over the next two millennia.

On the other hand, the whole New Testament is the history of the church written small. Everything that would happen to the Christian

---

37 Davies, R. E., *I Will Pour Out My Spirit* (Monarch Publications, 1992), pp. 48–50.

church in later centuries is there in the New Testament. The Acts of the Apostles opens with that unique outpouring of the Holy Spirit on the church at Pentecost. But from then on there were both the normal times of the church's life and the special occasions. When we read in Acts 4:31, 'After they prayed, the place where they were meeting was shaken. And they were all filled with the Holy Spirit and spoke the word of God boldly', we are compelled to ask, 'If they were all filled with the Holy Spirit now, what were they like five minutes before?' Here was a fuller experience of the power and presence of God than the disciples had enjoyed immediately before this.

As the New Testament story unfolds, churches embraced wrong doctrines (Galatia), became divisive and superficial (Corinth), lost their love for God (Ephesus), slid into a sickly lukewarmness (Laodicea) and remained like children in their faith (Hebrews). In each case there was certainly a need for a fresh outpouring of the Spirit. Paul's command to be 'filled with the Spirit' (Ephesians 5:18) implies an experience of receiving more of the evidence and power of the presence of God. Similarly, his cry for personal revival is found in Philippians 3:10: 'I want to know Christ and the power of his resurrection and the fellowship of sharing in his sufferings.'

Pentecost and the expectation of revival

In chapter 1 we saw that the promise of the new covenant heralded a new understanding, a new experience, a new commission and a new authority with the coming of the Holy Spirit at Pentecost. However, Pentecost was not an end but a beginning. What the Spirit did at Pentecost was not his final throw, but rather it was what he began to do. Just as the Gospels record all that Jesus 'began to do and teach' (Acts 1:1), so Pentecost heralded the continuation of that work by a new beginning.

If the expectation of Joel 2:28–32 was for a great outpouring of the Holy Spirit, and its fulfilment was Acts 2, then Pentecost is the great revival anticipated by the Old Testament prophets. However, Pentecost was a unique work of God in that many of its features could never be repeated. It was unquestionably a powerful outpouring of the Holy Spirit when one hundred and twenty disciples were saturated with God. At Pentecost, three thousand people from all over the Roman Empire, and beyond, came to Christ. This was God 'launching' his church. But the Pentecost experience was not the end. Strictly speaking it cannot be repeated, any more than the crucifixion can be repeated; to describe Acts 8 as the 'Samaritan pentecost' is therefore only loosely accurate.

Whilst Pentecost was a unique initiation of the new work of the Spirit, it was nevertheless a template by which revival can be measured. All the ingredients that we discovered in the Old Testament revivals were present on the day of Pentecost. It began with leaders who had a desperate longing for God and set themselves to pray (Acts 1:12–14; 2:1), and it ended as a people's movement (2:44–47). Pentecost was also marked by a diligent application to the word of God, a deep conviction of sin and a desire for holiness. All this is plain from Acts 2:40–47. The work of the Spirit transformed worship and its effect was evident to the surrounding neighbourhood. There was an awareness of God that filled everyone with awe. The new converts were also committed to the preaching of the apostles, and the whole life of the early church was modelled by the word of God. Pentecost initiated the largest and fastest gospel migration in the long history of the church; evangelism was an inevitable result of disciple making.

Like times of revival in the Old Testament, the immediate effect of Pentecost did not last beyond the first generation. In fact, it did not last too far into that first generation of Christians. Within a few decades there was need for a fresh work of the Spirit among the churches as the letters to the churches in Revelation 2 and 3 clearly reveal. However, because that generation takes us virtually to the end of the New Testament, we would not expect to read much about revival before the close of the canon of Scripture. It is all the more significant therefore when we discover indications of promises and prayers for revival.

God has never allowed his people to live in permanent revival. Revival is a time when God spoils his people by giving them all that they ask for and more. But God does not spoil his people for long. The church would not be strong if it was always in revival. The disciples in that upper room were a desperately dispirited group and nothing less than revival could 'launch' the church for the fulfilment of the great commission. But the normal life of the church is tough. It was easy, even though costly, to evangelize after Pentecost when the whole atmosphere was charged with the presence of God, but it would not be like that for long. The normal days of the church are a training time when God will test how easily the church can be drawn aside to the counterfeit, the odd and the ridiculous.

> The normal days of the church are a training time when God will test how easily the church can be drawn aside to the counterfeit, the odd and the ridiculous

Acts 3:19–22

Because Pentecost was what the Holy Spirit *began* to do, Peter introduced his hearers to a clear expectation of revival in the New Testament. In Acts 3:19–22 Peter was preaching in Jerusalem, perhaps only a few days after Pentecost. In the course of his sermon he made an important promise:

'Repent, then, and turn to God, so that your sins may be wiped out, that *times of refreshing* may come from the Lord, and that he may send the Christ, who has been appointed for you—even Jesus. He must remain in heaven until the time comes for God to restore everything, as he promised long ago through his holy prophets.'

Peter's command was for repentance, and then followed a three-fold promise: forgiveness, 'times of refreshing', and the Second Coming of Christ. In these verses we can hear an echo of Deuteronomy 30:2–3: 'When you and your children return to the Lord your God and obey him with all your heart and with all your soul according to everything I command you today, then the Lord your God will restore your fortunes and have compassion on you and gather you again from all the nations where he scattered you.' In Acts 2:38-39 we have the same echo, 'Repent, and let every one of you be baptized in the name of Jesus Christ for the remission of sins; and you shall receive the gift of the Holy Spirit. For the promise is to you and to your children, and to all who are afar off, as many as the Lord our God will call.'

That phrase 'times of refreshing' in Acts 3:19 is highly significant. The noun from which the word 'refreshing' comes means 'a breathing space or refreshment'; the verb can simply mean 'to recover one's breath, be refreshed or revived'. In its context here, the word primarily refers to spiritual revival.

There are two Greek words to denote time, although they are often used interchangeably: *chronos* frequently refers to time in general (in our time) whereas *kairos*, which is used here, refers to a particular period of time during which an event takes place. Here it is in the plural (times). It could be used of a season of opportunity, but it could also refer to a specific period of time.[38] The two words are used together in Acts 1:7, where the first word 'times' is *chronos* and the second word, 'seasons' is *kairos*. Exactly the same expression and order is used by Paul (deliberately?) in 1 Thessalonians 5:1 'times and dates'.

In Acts 3 the word is plural, so the promise of this 'refreshing' is for an indefinite number of 'seasons' or 'occasions'. The particular verbal

---

38 See Moulton and Milligan, *Vocabulary of the Greek New Testament* (Hendrickson Publishers, Oct 1997 orig. one vol. ed. 1930).

form of the word translated 'may come', is also interesting because it is exactly the same form as that translated in the next verse by 'He may send the Christ'.[39] The use of the word 'may' in modern translations is not intended to convey doubt and the *Authorized Version* in not incorrect by employing the word 'shall'. There is nothing doubtful about the fact of Christ's return, though for us the timing is uncertain. In the same way, times of refreshing (revival) are as certain as the return of Christ in that they will happen, but as uncertain as the return of Christ as to when they will happen. The verb in each case focuses on the event, or season, itself, without any hint as to how long it will continue or how often it will occur.

Commentators are in disagreement over what these 'times' refers to. But it ought not to be too difficult. Peter is clearly looking beyond Pentecost, which was certainly the initiation of 'the promise of the Father' (Acts 1:4), but that was behind him by Acts 3. He is now holding out a promise for the future. It lies between repentance, forgiveness and the return of Christ— and will be repeated. His promise is therefore: repentance, forgiveness, seasons of revival, and finally the return of Christ. Peter is as certain that there will be times of revival in the history of the church as he is that Christ will come again from heaven. But he does not know when such times will be or how long they will last. That is exactly what we concluded about the Old Testament prophets; they believed in any-time revival, but they did not know when, they did not know for how long, and they did not know how often.

An illustration of the unexpected nature of revival may be found in Acts 4:31. This was a new time of refreshing by the Holy Spirit for the disciples. The place where they were meeting was shaken 'and they were all filled with the Holy Spirit, and they spoke the word of God with boldness.' We cannot suggest that they were lukewarm and backsliding prior to this, but here is a new outpouring of the Spirit of God upon them that could only

---

39 It is the form known as the second aorist subjunctive.

be described as a new infilling of the Holy Spirit. The place where they were was physically shaken and they spoke with a renewed boldness. That is a powerful description of what we would understand today as revival.

What happened at Samaria in Acts 8 and in the house of Cornelius in Acts 10 may or may not be properly described as revival. Our decision on this will depend to upon whether or not we are prepared to accept that revival can sometimes begin among unbelievers. We have seen that it did at Nineveh in the time of Jonah. If the Ephesians described in Acts 19 were untaught Christians, then their experience can only be described as a spiritual revival.

Just as Old Testament revivals can be described as pre-Pentecost pentecosts, so all outpourings of the Spirit in fulfilment of Peter's promise are post-Pentecost pentecosts. This is not meant to detract from the uniqueness of Pentecost, any more than the sacrifices of the old covenant and the application of the atonement of Christ to a sinner today, detract from the uniqueness of the cross. Pentecost, like Golgotha, was a once-for-all occasion in history, the results of which are freely available today. Every person 'born-again' can be described as a personal Pentecost, just as each converted sinner has his own personal Golgotha encounter. But the promise of Peter offers something bigger and more widespread than a personal pentecost. He expects times when the Spirit would come in the manner of Pentecost itself.

Paul's prayers for revival

Paul's prayers are remarkable. That he worried over the churches daily and prayed for them regularly he admits (2 Corinthians 11:28; Philippians 1:4), but unlike so much of our vague praying today, Paul was specific. He frequently told the churches exactly what he wanted for them, and his requests fitted precisely their needs; they were tailored to the situation that he knew to be current in each church. For this reason, their content must tell us something about the needs of each church. More than this,

Paul's prayers were big prayers. The things he prayed for would transform the life of the church, and consequently they give us some idea of Paul's expectation of a new lease of life for the church, a renewal of spiritual vigour. We will consider just two of his prayers.

EPHESIANS 1:15–21; 3:14–21

Nowhere better does Paul reveal an expectation of new life for the church than in his letter to the church at Ephesus. In the first passage he prays for three things: a spirit of wisdom and revelation so that they might know God, an enlightened heart so that they might know the hope to which God had called them, and an enlightened heart so that they might know his incomparably great power.

It might seem strange that only ten years after the birth of the church in the most important city in the Roman province of Asia, Paul should think it necessary to pray that they might 'know God'. The word 'better', added by some translations (1:17 NIV) is an intrusion into the text—Paul did not write that. In 1526 William Tyndale well conveyed the meaning of this phrase in his translation: 'That God … might give you the Spirit of wisdom and open to you the knowledge of himself.' Already, in this affluent city with a thousand distractions, including a huge amphitheatre and the magnificent temple of Diana which was the envy of the Roman world, Paul could see that their first love and enthusiasm was beginning to wane. An early echo of a repeated problem (Revelation 2:4).

So far, this is a prayer that could be answered without the presence of what we understand as revival, but the reference to 'his incomparably great power' ('the working of his mighty power'(ESV), prepares us for the even bigger prayer of chapter 3:

'I pray that out of his glorious riches he may strengthen you with power through his Spirit in your inner being, so that Christ may dwell in your hearts through faith. And I pray that you, being rooted and established in love, may have power, together with all the saints, to grasp how wide and long and high and deep is the love of Christ, and to know this love that surpasses knowledge—that you may be filled to the measure of all the fullness of God.'

To know the width, length, height and depth of something provides us with all the dimensions we need to find out anything else that we may wish to know. And when we add to this the in-filling—whether by that knowledge or by the Spirit, Paul does not say—'to the measure of all the fullness of God', we have an expectation by Paul that is beyond our comprehension.

It is for this reason that the apostle continues with his doxology: 'Now to him who is able to do immeasurably more than all we ask or imagine, according to his power that is at work within us, to him be glory in the church and in Christ Jesus throughout all generations, for ever and ever! Amen.' The 'immeasurably more than all we ask or imagine' is clearly not a request for spiritual power for signs and wonders to startle the church and neighbourhood with unimaginable tricks of the supernatural. On the contrary, it is a prayer that the Ephesians might be so filled with the Spirit that they would experience 'the love of Christ' until they were 'filled with the fullness of God'. That last expression is almost inexplicable—which is presumably what Paul intended.

Paul was praying for an understanding and experience well beyond what the Ephesians currently knew. If any church or churches today were recipients of the answer to this prayer, they would undoubtedly be experiencing revival. The agency of this renewal of life is the Holy Spirit— 'the power that works in us'. This is a mind-blowing request by Paul.

Notice how he begins with something that we can handle. First, he wants us to be 'strengthened with might through his Spirit'; we can understand that and long for it. But Paul wants it to be a power that will enable us to grasp all there is concerning the love of God. That is an overwhelming love, so Paul wants us to be saturated—inundated—with

God. At this point the prayer is already beyond us. Just as our minds are struggling to grasp how big this might be, Paul adds that this is not all that he wants. He is also asking God to do 'immeasurably more than all we ask or imagine'. Still he has not finished, because the apostle is asking God to do this 'according to [which means 'in proportion to'] the power that works in us'.

Only in eternity will we begin to grasp the full import of a prayer like this. Meanwhile, is there a better description of what revival is than the answer to this prayer? Clearly the Ephesians were not experiencing all this, but equally clearly, they could. And Paul wanted them to. He was also convinced that it was within the sovereign hand of God to give, or else he would not have prayed such a prayer. This is Paul building upon the expectations of 'times of refreshing … from the Lord'. Like the prophets and Peter before him, Paul believed that there was always more that God could do for his people and that he was an any-time reviving God. In times of revival people are overwhelmed by the love of God, and it is commonly agreed that at such times the power of the Spirit is unexpected, unimaginable and inexpressible. That is precisely Paul's prayer here.

COLOSSIANS 1:9–12

Paul had never been to Colosse and therefore we might expect his prayer for the church there to be general. In fact, it is possibly the most profound and compound prayer in the Bible. In the Greek there are nearly eighty words in verses 9–12 but only three sentences. In all, there are two main clauses each of which has two subordinate clauses, and each of these is further qualified. There are eight separate statements in four verses! The grammatical construction of these verses is particularly complicated, and most commentators admit to being a little baffled by it. It is perhaps the best example of Paul's mind in overdrive.

In this prayer Paul was motivated by a good cause. The Christians at Colosse were known particularly for two things: 'faith in Christ Jesus and

… the love you have for all the saints' (v. 4). They had learned the gospel from Epaphras (v. 7), and the work was progressing most satisfactorily (v. 6). It was the success of the gospel that was the cause of Paul's prayer (v. 9). He was anxious to build upon success. The significance of this is that Paul was not praying for an ailing church. Although the Colossians had to be on their guard against 'deceptive philosophy' (2:8), the church was vigorous, healthy and growing; the quality of its life was well-known. However, Paul was never a man to be complacent; where there was life he wanted more life, and where there was growth he wanted more growth. Not only the church in decline can pray for revival.

Paul's two main prayers for this church were that God would 'fill you with the knowledge of his will' (v. 9) and that they would be 'strengthened with all power' (v. 11). But, as with the church at Ephesus, the knowledge and power were not for domestic entertainment. Paul wanted them to experience 'spiritual wisdom and understanding' and 'power, according to [God's] glorious might', so that they would live lives that were '*worthy* of the Lord' (the word *axios* means of equivalent weight or equal value) and fully pleasing to the Lord. Paul describes this as 'being fruitful in every good work' and 'increasing in the knowledge of God' (v. 10).

The key to all of this is that the church might be 'strengthened with all power, according to his glorious might' (v. 11). What Paul actually says here is, 'empowered with all power according to the dominion of his glory'; here the word for 'power' (*dunamis*), which is repeated, refers to the inherent power of God, and the word for 'might' (*kratos*) refers to his manifested power. In the first century this word was often used with reference to the gods or emperors,[40] and both Paul and Peter (1 Peter 4:11 'power') unashamedly turn it to Christian use. The inherent power of God is seen (manifested) in the creation and the resurrection, in both of

---

40 For example: 'the 38th year of the dominion of Caesar, son of the god'. Moulton and Milligan, *Vocabulary of the Greek New Testament*.

which the Holy Spirit was an active agent (Genesis 1:2 and 1 Peter 3:18). However, Paul makes it clear that in the case of the Christians at Colosse he is praying that the inherent power of the Spirit would be manifested in their 'great endurance ... patience and [joy]' (v. 11).

What has all this to do with revival? That this is a 'big' prayer is undeniable. How far the church at Colosse received the full benefit of God answering Paul's prayer on their behalf is not known to us. The fact that Colosse is not one of the churches mentioned in the seven letters of the apostle John (Revelation 2–3) could imply their continued steady growth. However, whether or not God answered Paul's prayer, this was certainly the apostle's longing for them; and the result intended would have been a new breath of life to a young church.

Unknown to Paul, within a few years of his letter the whole area around this city would be devastated by an earthquake, and their quality of endurance, patience and joy would be severely tested. The world around would soon see whether these Christians pleased their Lord and bore fruit in every good work. Perhaps, unknowingly, Paul's prayer was a preparation for what was to follow. Historically, revival often precedes a time of persecution or suffering.[41]

What must be clear is that Paul knew the size of his prayer and was aware that if God answered, it would transform the life of even this vigorous and healthy church. Although it is generally true that, as we have seen, when revival comes it comes primarily to a church that is in a weak state of decline, both the Bible and history show that there are exceptions. It is foolish for the healthy church to assume that it has all that it needs of God. There is a place in the life of every church to plead with God for more knowledge of himself and a greater experience of his Holy Spirit. And there is a good reason for this. How a church judges its own spiritual condition is almost always relative to its contemporary scene. No doubt

41 See *Revival—a people saturated with God*, pp. 246–250.

the church at Colosse could think of itself with satisfaction if it looked at the churches in Galatia or Corinth. But Paul knew better. He was aware that even the church at Colosse could go on to a deeper and higher quality of life and experience of God.

The Victorian preacher, C. H. Spurgeon, wisely commented that, in a healthy church: 'Their piety ought to need no reviving.' He went on to urge that such a church 'should aspire to a higher blessing, a richer mercy, than a mere revival. They should be asking for growth in grace, for increase of strength, and for greater success.' Perhaps Spurgeon makes a valid point: revival and maturity do not always go hand in hand; a revived church must long and pray for maturity— and this is precisely the point at which many revivals in history have ended in failure. A contented dissatisfaction should be the hallmark of even the healthiest church. Mere contentment will lead to complacency—the very thing for which, years later, the church at Ephesus was accused (Revelation 2:1–7) and even more so the church at Laodicea (Revelation 3:14–22).

> A contented dissatisfaction should be the hallmark of even the healthiest church. Mere contentment will lead to complacency

The need of the first-century church for revival

Before the close of the New Testament there were many churches across Asia that were certainly in desperate need of revival. From the second and third chapters of Revelation that much is clear. The warning of the Spirit to the outwardly healthy church at Ephesus is this:

'Yet I hold this against you: You have forsaken your first love. Remember the height from which you have fallen! Repent and do the things you did at first. If you do not repent, I will come to you and remove your lampstand from its place' (Revelation 2:4–5).

The Ephesian church enjoyed some of those very qualities that Paul included in his prayer for the church at Colosse: it was hard-working, enduring, patient and holy. It looked excellent. Yet in reality the church had become spiritually dry. A church like this surely needs fresh life and vitality—a 'season of refreshing'. And this new life would begin with repentance. God's offer was that if they turned to him, there would be something far better for them.

The Spirit gave a similar warning to the church at Pergamum. Their loyalty under persecution in the past (Revelation 2:13) could not disguise the fact that they had allowed the Nicolaitans to settle in the church and spread the devastating doctrine of compromise with pagan religion and morality. This could be compared only to the false prophet Balaam in the Old Testament (vv. 14–15). Their journey into the blessing of God must also begin with repentance (v. 16).

The church at Sardis was ordered to 'Wake up! Strengthen what remains and is about to die' (3:2). Its condition was perilous; it had a reputation for spiritual life but in reality was spiritually as good as dead. God saw through their veneer and urged them to come alive to the reality of their situation before it was too late. Here was a church in urgent need of a time of refreshing, and the command was for them to 'remember ... and repent' (3:3).

Two churches were given no command to repent with the offer of new life in return. The church at Smyrna (2:8–11) was the only church among the seven that was offered no respite from the relentless persecution which they had been facing so bravely. Thyatira, on the other hand, appears to have been hi-jacked by the spiritual descendants of Jezebel and there remained only judgement for these people and an encouragement for the faithful to 'hold on to what you have until I come' (2:25). Perhaps there is a hint of widespread gospel success to the church at Philadelphia—which would be kept 'from the hour of trial' (3:10)—in the promise that their persecutors would 'fall down at your feet and acknowledge that I have loved you' (v. 9).

The most notorious church that was in need of spiritual reviving was the church at Laodicea. These Christians were proud of their city, confident of their spirituality and ignorant of their real condition. The Spirit described them as 'lukewarm, and neither cold nor hot … [you] do not know that you are wretched, pitiful, poor, blind and naked' (3:16–17). They were counselled to seek God earnestly and in repentance, in order to gain true spiritual wealth, holiness and enlightenment (gold, white garments and eye-salve). The picture here of Christ standing outside his church and pleading for admission, together with the promise of banqueting with his people, must refer to the radical contrast in their spiritual life before and after revival. This is a clear invitation by the Lord of the church for them to return in repentance and plead with God for spiritual revival. For all the sermons based on the letter to the church at Laodicea, churches today have rarely taken either its warnings or its promises seriously.

> For all the sermons based on the letter to the church at Laodicea, churches today have rarely taken either its warnings or its promises seriously

Perhaps the most intriguing fact about the letters to the seven churches is the nature of the promises that are offered to them. Most of the churches are offered promises that will clearly be fulfilled at the end of time. To Ephesus the promise of eating of 'the tree of life, which is in the paradise of God' (2:7) is apparently an end-of-time reward; which means that the only stated promise to this church is that God will not remove their witness (lampstand) so long as they repent (v. 5). The crown of life offered to the faithful at Smyrna (2:10) and the authority over the nations promised to Thyatira (2:26) may equally be end-time promises. The same can be said of the promises to Sardis (3:4–5).

However, at least three churches are given an expectation of a change in their circumstances here on earth. The Philadelphians will be kept from imminent persecution, and some of the other promises to them may have a fulfilment in their own day (3:9–10). The Laodiceans, of whom the Spirit had nothing positive to record, are offered the privilege of new spiritual life and the Lord returning to his church in an intimate friendship (3:18, 20). It is a matter of debate how far the 'hidden manna' offered to Pergamum (2:17) is a spiritual refreshment rather than something only to be gained in the age to come. In view of their confrontation with pagan feasts, it is very likely that the manna referred to here is the presence of the Lord himself among his people.

Beyond the different circumstances and spiritual conditions of these churches lies the fact that the Spirit's offer of remedial action was also different. Some were told to repent and were offered new life in return; others were given no such offer of a refreshing. Some were in need of spiritual revival and were offered it—though the word 'revival' was not used. Others, like Smyrna, might have longed for just such a respite from their painful experience but were simply commanded to 'hold on'. All this reveals the sovereign Lord of the church dispensing to his people as he plans and not always as they might desire. What is clear is that most of these churches were being offered new life in return for the old—if they repented, corrected their failures and returned to the Lord. That is an offer of revival.

In summary, the possibility of any-time revival is more evident in the New Testament than is often appreciated. Pentecost is certainly understood as the fulfilment of Old Testament promises, and in that sense it is the greatest and most significant outpouring of the Spirit on the church. But it is not the last one. The Spirit came repeatedly upon the church in Jerusalem and elsewhere, and this was precisely what Peter prophesied during his sermon in Solomon's porch at the temple. Paul's prayers assumed the willingness of God to bless his church by the Spirit in almost inexpressible—because unimaginable—ways, and the promises of the Spirit to the churches in Asia towards the end of the first century were based equally upon the assumption that revival was a possibility following repentance. The clear revival expectation of the prophets throughout the old covenant is no less the anticipation of the apostles throughout the new.

7. Expectation of revival in the history of the church

There can be little doubt that throughout the prophets there are promises of spiritual renewal which cannot be understood in any other way than revival. Isaiah 41:17–20 and Hosea 14:4–7 are two of many well-known prophecies. The question is, when are these to be fulfilled? Could such a time be expected in the prophet's own day? Are they limited to the age of the Messiah? Or are they reserved as a beautiful description of the new heavens and the new earth?

We cannot avoid the subject of interpreting Old Testament prophecy. It is not sufficient to ransack the Old Testament in a hunt for any verse that appears to refer to revival, and then to hold it out as a promise that God is obliged to keep. God is not committed to keep a promise he has never made.

> God is not committed to keep a promise he has never made

Understanding the millennium!

The 'millennium' refers to the period of one thousand years that is mentioned in the book of Revelation 20:2 and 7. An angel 'seized the dragon, that ancient serpent, who is the devil, or Satan, and bound him for a thousand years ... When the thousand years are over, Satan will be released from his prison and will go out to deceive the nations in the four corners of the earth.'

There are three main approaches to understanding this 'one thousand years' (millennium). However, there are a range of views within each of these positions broadly outlined:

The *postmillennial* view believes that before Christ comes there will be a period (either a literal or symbolic one thousand years) of universal revival, a golden age of gospel success. Because the belief is that Christ will finally return *after* this millennium, it is known as *post*millennialism. This golden age may come progressively as a slow build-up of gospel success, or it may come as a sudden glorious revival.

The *premillennial* view holds that Christ will come in glory and establish an earthly kingdom centred upon Jerusalem. For one thousand years he will reign as king and there will be a mass conversion of the Jews. Christ will therefore come *before* the millennium in order to establish his thousand years of earthly rule. That is why it is known as *pre*millennialism.

Amillennialism maintains that the thousand years is a symbol of the period of the gospel age from Christ's ascension right up to the end of time—to the point where Christ comes to end the present age and establish his new heavens and new earth.

Understanding prophecy

What you have just read is a simplistic way of explaining the millennial positions. Where this affects our understanding of Old Testament prophecy can be seen if we take *Isaiah 35* as an example.

'The desert and the parched land will be glad; the wilderness will rejoice and blossom. Like the crocus, it will burst into bloom; it will rejoice greatly and shout for joy. The glory of Lebanon will be given to it, the splendour of Carmel and Sharon; they will see the glory of the LORD, the splendour of our God. Strengthen the feeble hands, steady the knees that give way; say to those with fearful hearts, "Be strong, do not fear; your God will come, he will come with vengeance; with divine retribution he will come to save you." Then will the eyes of the blind be opened and the ears of the deaf unstopped. Then will the lame leap like a deer, and the mute tongue shout for joy. Water will gush forth in the wilderness and streams in the desert. The burning sand will become a pool, the thirsty ground bubbling springs. In the haunts where jackals once lay, grass and reeds and papyrus will grow. And a highway will be there; it will be called the Way of Holiness. The unclean will not journey on it; it will be for those who walk in that Way; wicked fools will not go about on it. No lion will be there, nor will any ferocious beast get up on it; they will not be found there. But only the redeemed will walk there, and the ransomed of the LORD will return. They will enter Zion with singing; everlasting joy will crown their heads. Gladness and joy will overtake them, and sorrow and sighing will flee away.'

This may be taken as a poetic description of the golden age of revival before Christ finally returns (postmillennial), a beautiful poetic picture of the millennial rule of Christ on earth prior to the end of the age (premillennial), or symbolic of the age of the gospel now or, more generally, of the ultimate kingdom of God at the end of time (amillennial).

All this may be very confusing—even discouraging—and therefore when we come to an Old Testament passage it is easy to conclude that with all these options it is not worth making the effort. Since commentators are far from agreed among themselves, how can we know? During the history of the Christian church those three main millennial views have been tossed back and forth with the emphasis sometimes on one and then on another.

The postmillennial view

Many of the Puritans believed in a postmillennial future, expecting a time of universal revival before the final return of Christ. They anticipated the conversion of the Jews, though not in a premillennial kingdom ruled by Christ on earth. They expected the steady progress of the gospel through periodic revivals to be so successful that countless millions of Jews and

Gentiles all over the world would be brought to Christ. The whole earth would be full of the knowledge of the Lord as the waters cover the sea (Isaiah 11:9; Habakkuk 2:14). However, earlier reformers in the sixteenth century, such as Luther and Calvin, did not expect either a great conversion of the Jews or a golden age of success; some of the Puritans in the seventeenth century shared their view, notably Richard Baxter of Kidderminster.

Some of the best Puritans, John Owen and Thomas Goodwin among them, met in London in 1658. They represented the Independents and Congregationalists, and *The Savoy Declaration* included a clear statement of their expectation of a time of universal revival before the return of Christ.[42] Many Presbyterian Puritans, like Thomas Manton, David Dickson and Samuel Rutherford, identified themselves with this view. This was certainly the position of the American pastor and theologian, Jonathan Edwards: 'It is evident from the Scripture, that there is yet remaining a great Advancement of the Interest of Religion and the Kingdom of Christ in this World, by an abundant outpouring of the Spirit of God, far greater and more extensive than ever yet has been.'[43] Many Scottish ministers joined him in this conviction.

This position continued to be held well into the nineteenth century by men like Robert Murray M'Cheyne in Scotland. One example of the postmillennial position is found in a series of lectures which were given in Glasgow in 1840 and which were published under the title *The Revival of Religion*.[44] The theme is best seen in the contribution of John G. Lorimer in Lecture 8 entitled 'Encouragements from the Promises and Prophecies

---

42 *The Savoy Declaration*, Ch. 26, *Of the church*.
43 Edwards set out his position in a lengthy treatise: *An Humble Attempt To promote Explicit Agreement and Visible union of God's People in Extraordinary Prayer For the revival of Religion and the Advancement of Christ's Kingdom on Earth, pursuant to Scripture-Promises and Prophecies concerning the last Time*. With a preface by several Ministers. Boston, New-England 1747. See below, pp. 186 ff.
44 Edited by W. M. Hetherington and republished by the Banner of Truth Trust in 1984.

of Scripture'. Lorimer was answering the question: 'How can we be encouraged to pray for revival?' His confident answer is that Scripture prophecies encourage us to believe that revival is inevitable towards the end of time. Lorimer asserted that the word of God 'teems ... with assurances and prophecies of a day of coming universal religious revival.'

A similar optimism was found in America during the revivals of the early part of the nineteenth century. Two years before Lorimer delivered his lecture in Glasgow, Calvin Colton was typical of many when he analysed revivals in America and wrote enthusiastically about the future. Condemning those who looked forward pessimistically, Colton encouraged his readers to expect the church 'to march directly to the conquest of the world' by a 'perpetual revival of religion—a revival without a consequent decline—an outpouring of the Spirit not to be withdrawn, or relaxed, so as to bring in all ... of every community and every nation'.[45] Edward Griffin, president of Williams College in New England and the evangelist Asahel Nettleton took the same view.

It is clear therefore how important revivals are to those holding a postmillennial position, and consequently how important it is that they can find the promise of revivals in the Old Testament. Before the church arrives at the great end-time revival, it will require a series of revivals *en route*. It was uncertain whether the millennium was literally a thousand years or symbolic of a fixed period of time known only to God.

The premillennial view

During the nineteenth century a shift took place in favour of premillennialism. This can be illustrated by an event that happened in May 1828. Edward Irvine, a flamboyant and eloquent preacher, decided to give twelve early morning lectures, the subject of which was 'The Apocalypse'.

---

45 Calvin Colton, *History and Character of American revivals of Religion* (Westley and Davis, London 1838), pp. 141, 195–6. Quoted in Lovelace, *Dynamics of Spiritual Life*, pp. 401–402.

Chapter 7

It was an attempt to reassert premillennialism. The occasion Irvine chose was the General Assembly of the Church of Scotland in Edinburgh. He had no authority to give such lectures, and as he did not want to clash with any of the assembly meetings, he decided to hold his lectures at six o'clock in the morning. He obtained the use of a large church in the city and he packed it; he chose a bigger one and that also was filled. Even Dr Chalmers, with whom Irvine had previously worked as an assistant, was unable to get in. During those lectures Andrew and Horatius Bonar were converted to premillennialism.

Irvine's twelve lectures to the crowded congregations at St Cuthbert's contained a spirited defence of premillennial hopes coupled with some strange uses of Old Testament prophecy. Daniel's fourth beast, who was given the power to 'think to change times and laws' (Daniel 7:25, AV), was confidently reckoned as a prophecy of the British Government's current attempt to repeal the Test Act! Few fully understood Irvine's theology, but it could be said of Irvine just as it was once said of the rhetoric of Queen Elizabeth I: 'Whilst no one could say exactly what she meant, everybody agreed it was worth listening to.'

Edward Irvine's personal story is a sad one. Sincere in his search for God, he became an extreme charismatic yet was never able to speak in the 'tongues' he so longed for, and many of his prophecies failed. Eventually Irvine lost all credibility and support.[46] However, he had presented the subject in a popular style and a drift towards premillennialism gathered momentum. During the nineteenth century, the published teaching of John Nelson Darby, the founder of the Plymouth Brethren movement, advanced the cause even more in Britain. Mixed in with this resurgence of premillennialism was a measure of 'dispensationalism' aided by the notes

---

46 A careful study of his life is found in Arnold Dallimore, *The Life of Edward Irvine* (Banner of Truth Trust, 1983).

in the Schofield Bible. In this view all history can be divided into neat periods of prophetic fulfilment.

Premillennial views were especially popular among evangelical Christians during the last half of the nineteenth and the first half of the twentieth century. Premillennialism did not need to lay such stress upon the necessity for revival, because the millennial kingdom of Christ will come when Christ returns as King. When he comes, he will establish his kingdom so that he can personally superintend the affairs of his earthly rule. For premillennialism, revivals—desirable though they may be—form no *necessary* part of the end-of-time (eschatological) hope.

Unsurprisingly, during the last half of the nineteenth century to the first half of the twentieth century the urgency of prayer for revival was to some extent lessened. There were some outstanding revivals during that period—in Wales in 1904 and East Anglia in 1921 for example—but the tendency was to refocus. We were not now expecting a marvellous golden age or a continual progress towards this glorious gospel success; on the contrary, the church looked for a time when Christ would come and establish a kingdom over which he would reign and from which he would superintend all the affairs of his kingdom on earth. To many therefore, revival was less important than the hope of the millennial kingdom of Christ.

One effect of both the post-millennium and pre-millennium understanding of Scripture is that the Old Testament prophecies and the New Testament promises of an outpouring of the Spirit are locked into either the end of time golden age or the millennial kingdom. This leaves little Scripture left for an expectation of intermediate revivals. One contemporary American author, for example, reserves the prophetic promises and Acts 3:19 for the coming millennial age.[47]

---

47 MacArthur J. F., *Acts* (Moody Press, Chicago 1994). Vol. 1, pp. 118–120.

Chapter 7

The amillennial view

Partly as a reaction to some of the literalism of premillennialism in its interpretation of Old Testament prophecy and to some of the bizarre applications like those of Irvine and his followers, amillennialism received a growing interest during the middle of the twentieth century. When William Hendriksen first published his commentary on the book of Revelation in 1939, it ran against the tide of popular evangelical opinion.[48] The 'Definite and sane principles of interpretation', which were claimed for Henriksen's book, became popular over the next few decades and amillennialism received strong support among younger evangelicals in the United Kingdom. However, it should be noted that pre-millennialism was the mainstream position in the United States—and still is. Under the amillennial view, many Old Testament prophecies were seen as referring to the age of the gospel rather than necessary promises of revival or of the millennium. At least it was a strong antidote to what is referred to as 'The many fantastic explanations that have cluttered around this scriptural gem'—the Book of Revelation.[49]

The swing of the pendulum

A new movement swung the pendulum once more. The rise of the charismatic renewal movement from the late 1960s saw a slow return to a postmillennial expectation. At first many of those who adopted charismatic renewal assumed that revival had come. Evidence of the 'gifts' was seen as evidence of revival. For this reason, 'restoration' (of 'charismatic' gifts) and 'revival' became synonymous nouns. Recent years have cooled the enthusiasm of some who confused those two very different issues. Many charismatics who are driven by the existential philosophy of experience in preference to authority, saw such phenomena as the 'Toronto enthusiasm'

---

48 William Hendriksen, *More than Conquerors* (Baker Book House, 1939).
49 *More than Conquerors*, Preface.

first of all as a 'rumour of revival' and then as revival itself. In reality it was neither.

Millennial history produces some strange bedfellows. The modern charismatic renewal movement is largely postmillennial not premillennial; on this issue at least, many charismatics hold a prophetic view not too dissimilar from that of the Puritans in the seventeenth century and of their successors in the eighteenth and nineteenth centuries. An example of this is found in a charismatic magazine. Four articles appeared under the title 'Global revival', which is the kind of expression that the Puritans and men like Jonathan Edwards, Murray M'Cheyne and John Lorimer could have used. These articles gave a clear statement of a postmillennial hope. One writer closed with a reference to Zechariah 2:10–13 and with the words 'That is ultimate revival.'[50] Another writer added, 'It seems to me beyond question that the world is destined for a great and glorious revival in which multitudes will be swept into the Kingdom of God.'[51] He offered only Romans 11 and the final 'ingathering' of the Jews as Scripture proof of that hope, but at least he himself was convinced 'beyond question'. This postmillennialism lay behind the renewed interest in revival among many charismatic Christians.

In 1840 Lorimer had asked the question: 'But how will the church arrive at this glorious millennium?', and he provided the answer: 'The scripture seems to leave no room for doubt that there is to be the occasional outbreakings of sudden and singular revival.' However, he offered no scripture for this.[52] Lorimer believed that we need such outpourings because each wave of revival will advance the church. In other words, each revival will build on the one before and take the church a step further towards this glorious golden age of success.

---

50 *Restoration* for September/October,1989.
51 *Restoration*, p.93.
52 *The Revival of Religion*, pp.202–203.

But does history teach us that each revival builds on the advances of the previous one? The reign of Manasseh followed on from the revival under Hezekiah, and in half a century Manasseh undid all that was achieved during that revival and the nation was worse at the end of Manasseh's reign than it was at the beginning of Hezekiah's reign. When Josiah, Manasseh's son, came to the throne the people did not even know where the law of God was—they had lost their Bible.

We learn the same from the history of the church. Where today is the evidence of the 1814 revival in Cornwall or of the revival that swept down the Swaledale valley in Yorkshire in the middle of the nineteenth century— apart from scores of chapels that have been converted into private homes or now lie derelict? Where is the residue of the 1904 revival in Wales today apart from fond memories by a few? How widespread is the legacy of the 1921 revival in East Anglia and the eastern seaboard of Scotland? Even the fire of the 1949 and 50s revivals in the Western Isles of Scotland has sadly become a dying ember of diminishing heart religion. Admittedly, these are parochial examples, and it could be argued that the global picture is different. The Great Awakening that may be said to have begun at Hernhut in 1727, led to a dramatic increase in world evangelization; the Second Awakening that lasted from the end of the eighteenth century, led to the dynamic Victorian missionary movement. Nevertheless, there is little evidence today that God is building each wave of revival upon the previous one. Still less do we appear to be moving steadily towards a glorious goal of universal gospel success.

Lorimer concluded, 'We are entitled then to look for religious revivals in the future days of the church. They are essential to the fulfilment of prophecy. If there be no revivals the prophecy fails, and with its failure the evidence of Christianity is compromised.'[53] On that we may agree. We have seen that whilst we cannot specify when or how revival will come,

---

53 Above, p. 221.

undoubtedly the prophets and the promise in Acts and the expectation in the prayers of Paul give us strong biblical reason to call upon God to saturate his people with himself and so revive the cause of Christ in the world today.

8. Encouraging prayer for revival—using our Bible

An invitation at the church prayer meetings to pray for revival is often a sure way to invite silence.

Evangelical Christians today do not know what to pray for under that heading. This is perfectly understandable if a church has never been told what revival is, biblically and historically. However, many prayer meetings would take on a new purpose and dynamic if attention were drawn to the paradigm prayers of Paul, such as Ephesians and Colossians that we examined in chapter 6. To spend a few minutes understanding what Paul was expecting, and then pray his prayers as our own, may well receive answers that would be far more valuable than most of the things traditionally brought before God at our weekly prayer meetings. These model prayers in Ephesians and Colossians are there to help us.

To be convinced that revival is a thoroughly biblical experience which is found throughout both the Old and New Testaments, is only a first step—although a very important one. If, in the past, God has given his people this experience in their times of need, and if his character leads us to believe that it may be ours as often as we need it, plead for it, and he chooses to give it, then we are challenged to pray for it. But what does that mean in practice?

Hindrances to praying for revival

Today there are many reasons why Christians do not pray for revival. Some simply do not believe that revival is a biblical experience, others are cynical because they consider the subject has been overrated and overstated, others are afraid of the disorder that revival may bring and some are discouraged because, after much prayer, revival has not come—consistent disappointment reduces expectation. However, there are two other significant factors that have confused prayer for revival.

The first is **misdirection**. Too often we have been led to believe that a particular contemporary experience is evidence of the wind of revival blowing. The experience has come, changed shape and either diminished or disappeared. But the assertion that this is revival has satisfied many; unintentionally they have been content with a stone instead of the Spirit. It is not unbelieving to be cautious before we assert that any particular phenomenon is the wind of revival. To claim too much too often leads to widespread disillusion or shallow satisfaction. We either give up in despair or we are content with anything. Either way, prayer

> To claim too much too often leads to widespread disillusion or shallow satisfaction

for revival ceases. In his warning against Christians swallowing the culture of their day, Jim Packer suggests that many evangelicals are 'restless existentialists' [54]—the constant demand for experiences to bolster our religion.

Another hindrance concerns those who do pray for revival, but who use Scripture out of context. This is a **hermeneutical presumption**. 'Hermeneutics' is the interpretation of a passage of Scripture: how a passage should be understood and applied. By adding the word 'presumption' is meant that Christians sincerely seeking revival often lay claims before God that are biblically unfounded. Sometimes, passages from the Bible are used in revival prayer meetings that are misapplied, but from these passages we proceed to demand that God should keep his word. We have consequently

---

54 J. I. Packer, *A Quest for Godliness* (Crossways, Illinois). p. 30.

used the Bible as a mantra, in the expectation that simply the recitation of Scripture must have persuasive force with God. However, remember that God is not committed to keep promises he has not made.

To grasp the importance of this we must appreciate that there are two kinds of promise that God makes in Scripture: one is unconditional and specific and the other is conditional and either specific or general. The importance of this distinction is that if God does not keep his unconditional and specific promises then his honour and character are compromised; on the other hand, he will not keep a conditional promise unless the conditions are fulfilled. God gave specific and unconditional promises concerning the ancestry of the Saviour of the world and of Israel's return from exile. Consequently, if the Messiah had not come through the line of Abraham and David, or if Israel had not returned to Jerusalem under Cyrus of Persia after her years of exile, then the specific and unconditional promises of God would have failed. On the other hand, the promise in 2 Chronicles 7:14, 'If my people ... will humble themselves, and pray and seek my face...', is a conditioned promise that God gave to his chosen people Israel through Solomon; no specific occasion was in mind, but a condition had to be fulfilled. Provided they responded sincerely to the condition, Israel could claim the promise whenever they were in need. Because its fulfilment was not specifically located, how and when God responded would be wholly at his discretion.

This does not mean that 2 Chronicles 7:14 is out of bounds when the Christian prays for revival; on the contrary, God reveals a principle about his own character in this verse. The 'land' referred to is the land of Israel, and no Christians in any nation today can claim this as a promise for their own land. But we may use this verse in our appeal to God, not on the ground of a specific promise he has made and must fulfil, or even on the ground of a conditional promise that he must keep, providing we fulfil the conditions, but on the basis that this is a revelation of the kind of God he is: a forgiving and restoring God. *In other words we can plead on the basis of the principle rather than demand on the ground of a promise.* God would still be a forgiving and restoring God if, for his better purposes, he did not revive his people in response to their prayer. As an example of prayer based upon the character of God, we may pray earnestly for the salvation of a friend on the ground that God is merciful; but he is not bound to answer as we request, because mercy is only one aspect of his character.

In one Christian magazine a writer maintained, 'To release faith for revival I must find the basis for my prayer in the promises of God.'[55] In this he is right, but we must be sure that the areas of Scripture that we choose really are the promises of God. In the same magazine another contributor refers us to Matthew 13:24–43 and reasons that Christ's agricultural analogies lead us to believe there will be days before the final Day and harvests before the final Harvest at the end of the age. He concludes, 'It seems to me beyond question that the world is destined for a great and glorious revival in which multitudes will be swept into the kingdom of God.'[56] Doubtless that is his wishful hope, but he offers no adequate New Testament evidence to support it. It is certainly not discovered in Matthew 13, and the only other passage referred to is Romans 11 which, given the various interpretations of this chapter, can hardly be held as a promise 'beyond question' of ultimate end-time revival. In other words, the writer is holding God to a promise that he may never have made.

A third writer in this magazine commented on James 5:7–9 and 17–18, 'James implies that we ought to intercede for both autumn and spring rains before the Lord's coming.'[57] But that is not James' intention. The farmer is an illustration of waiting patiently for the Second Coming of the Lord, and Elijah is an illustration of praying in faith. Neither passage can be taken as a promise of a specific coming revival. It is hermeneutical presumption to suggest that a doctrine of periodic revival leading to a

55 Bryn Jones, *Restoration* Sept/Oct, 1989. p. 20.
56 Above, Tony Ling, p. 18.
57 Hugh Thompson. Above, pp. 16–17.

great end-time revival can be built upon James 5:7. Similarly Acts 15:13–18 is taken as the basis for the hope that, 'The world is destined for a great and glorious revival in which multitudes will be swept into the Kingdom of God.' The writer concludes that the use of Amos 9 in this passage is 'proof of a worldwide move of the Holy Spirit to gather men and women from every nation into the church of Jesus Christ.'[58] This is true in the sense of the steady work of the gospel throughout the history of the church, but in Acts 15 James simply uses Amos 9 to prove that God always intended to give the gospel to the elect Gentiles. To understand it as a specific promise of end-time revival is not an acceptable conclusion from Acts 15 or Amos 9. It is hermeneutical presumption.

This hermeneutical presumption has been widespread in the history of the church's longing for revival. When John Lorimer in the mid-nineteenth century used Luke 11:13, 'How much more will your Father in heaven give the Holy Spirit to those who ask him' as a promise of end-time revival, he too had slipped into the same fallacy. Certainly Luke 11:13 can be used in prayer for revival, but it does not contain a specific promise of a specific period of revival at a specific time in the history of the church. What it does give us is the right to remind God of his character as a gracious and giving Father who wants the best for his children—and the best is giving his Holy Spirit to us.

Lorimer claimed, 'The Word of God teems with ... assurances and prophecies of a day of coming universal religious revival.'[59] But in this context the only references he offers us are Psalms 22 and 72; Isaiah 54:1 and Jeremiah 3:17. Such a conclusion would never be discovered in the passages themselves. Some have coined the word *eisegesis* to describe this. *Exegesis* is correctly reading the meaning *out* of the passage, whilst *eisegesis* is reading our own meaning *into* the passage.

---

58 Tony Ling, p. 19.
59 *The Revival of Religion*, edited by W. M. Hetherington and republished by the Banner of Truth Trust in 1984, p. 188.

None of this is intended to whittle away the value of Scripture in our prayer for revival; on the contrary, the Bible will always remain our chief incentive and strongest plea with God when praying for revival. However, we must be sure whether our prayer is on the basis of God's unconditional promise of specific revival, his conditional promise of revival generally, or on the ground of what we know about his character as a revival-giving God.

Seven centuries before Pentecost, the prophet Hosea had much to teach about God's promise of revival to Israel and, based upon his character revealed here, it will strengthen our resolve in prayer and add force to our hope to 'move the hand that moves the world'.

Having removed two significant barriers to effective prayer for revival—*misdirection* and *hermeneutical presumption*—we are ready to examine a few passages of Scripture that we may use in our prayerful longing for revival in our own day. In the previous chapter we discovered just how large the prayers and expectations of Paul were for the first century churches and concluded that if ever we do not know how to pray as we should, those model prayers in Ephesians and Colossians would prove an excellent place to begin. We so rarely hear prayers that are grounded in Scripture.

Prayer, any prayer, is not simply a matter of letting God hear our voice. If we are serious about obtaining what we most long for, we must be sure of the ground on which we come. Do we have a biblical case to present to him? We must also be ready to respond in whatever way his word directs. The prophets knew that the people must put things right if they were to expect a response from God.

God listens to biblical prayers, not wishful mantras (Matthew 6:7). Simply to quote Scripture passages to God is no guarantee that they are relevant to our cause, still less that he

> God listens to biblical prayers, not wishful mantras

will listen and respond. We must pray them in context. There is no value in using just any passage of Scripture in prayer because it sounds good. We must understand firstly whether the passage, taken in its context, is relevant to our subject and secondly what we mean by each turn of phrase. The Bible is to be understood not just quoted—and applied not just believed. To think through each passage before we use it, to place it in its context and then to apply it to our own situation, is the only way to engage God's attention and press our case for revival.

Encouraging prayer for revival using our Bible

What follows are not full expositions but are intended simply as notes to put each passage in context and to highlight the important themes. They are cameos of prayer for revival, which could be used either privately or corporately as a preparation for praying for revival.

HOSEA 14:1-9—GOD IS READY TO HEAL WHEN WE ARE READY TO REPENT

Hosea began preaching a little earlier than Isaiah, in the days of King Uzziah of Judah (810–758 BC) and he continued for half a century or more. Jeroboam II of Israel led the north into a period of unprecedented prosperity (for some) and relative peace and security. After his death in 753 BC, a quick succession of the remaining six kings in the north led to Assyrian domination. Israel withheld tribute from Assyria and formed an alliance with the 'broken reed' of Egypt. In 722 BC Assyria invaded and destroyed Samaria and carried the cream of the population into exile. This chapter is addressed to Israel, the northern kingdom. The plea by Hosea for Israel to return in repentance apparently went unheeded.

God has already been pleading with Israel.
- Look at your sin: you have depended on yourself (10:13)
- Look at your history: my faithfulness and your unfaithfulness (11:1–4)
- Look at your future: without me you will suffer (11:5–6)
- Look at your empty religion: your words mean nothing to me (11:7)

- Look at my compassion for you: my heart is still towards you (11:8)
- Look at your preferred 'security': your king has not saved you (13:9–11)

Israel must acknowledge that their only help comes from God. He reminds them that they wanted to be like all the other nations. In our own day we are driven by methods of commerce, social science or psychology. To suggest a return to the Lord by renewing the prayer meeting would be considered by many too simplistic. So, we struggle on in our own 'success', which we measure by numbers, programmes and buildings. We will attend any conference that offers a new method.

Here, then is the prophet's plea.

Take words and return to the Lord (14:2–3). Not pious attitudes or wishful dreaming. The prophet provides the words for them: an admission of guilt, a plea for mercy, a rejection of empty worship, and an acknowledgement that our best schemes have failed us.

Then in 14:4–7, God responds by offering:

- a new spiritual life—their backsliding healed
- a new spiritual relationship—he will love them freely
- a new spiritual freedom—the anger of God turned away
- a new spiritual experience—God will be to them like dew

During the dry season from March to October the night mist provided sufficient moisture for life to bring:

- beauty (the lily v. 5)—Titus 2:10
- strength (cedars of Lebanon v. 5)—Ephesians 6:10
- royal honour (olive tree v. 6)—Revelation 1:6
- fragrance (cedars of Lebanon v. 6)—2 Corinthians 2:15
- security (shade of the cedars v. 7)—Romans 8:39
- life (grain v. 7)—John 10:10
- growth (the vine v. 7)—Ephesians 4:15
- endurance (a green cypress tree v. 8)—1 Corinthians 15:58
- fruitfulness (v. 8)—Romans 7:4

Verse 9. This is the way of wisdom. The plea may have passed unheeded by the north, but it was not without effect. Six years after the fall of Samaria, Hezekiah assumed the throne in Jerusalem and set himself to do all that Hosea had encouraged the northern kingdom to do—and revival followed (2 Chronicles 29–31).

For us, this passage does not provide the promise of revival at any particular time, but it does lay out many of the principles that we can apply to ourselves and many of the blessings that we can plead into a new covenant context. We are at liberty to remind God of the way he dealt with his people in the Old Testament—providing we are prepared to take notice of the warnings and correct our lives accordingly.

ISAIAH 63:15 TO 64:12—A CRY OF ANGUISH FOR REVIVAL[60]

Isaiah began his ministry 'In the year that King Uzziah died' (6:1; *c.*758 BC) and continued into the reign of Hezekiah—a period of at least forty years. He was therefore a contemporary of Hosea but, unlike Hosea who preached mainly to Israel, Isaiah's message ranged widely and, in addition to Judah, he prophesied against Israel in the north and most of the surrounding nations: Assyria, Babylonia, Philistia, Moab, Syria, Ethiopia, Egypt, Edom, Arabia and Tyre. The prosperity under Jeroboam II in the north was matched under Uzziah in the south, and with the same spiritual consequences. With the fall of Samaria in 722 BC Isaiah warned Jerusalem not to enter into alliances against Assyria and pleaded with the nation to return to God. The prophet lived through the period of revival in the time of Hezekiah (2 Chronicles 29 to 31) and played a significant role in the refusal of Hezekiah and Jerusalem to capitulate to Sennacherib of Assyria (Isaiah 36 to 37).

---

60 In *The Turn of the Tide* (Heath Trust, Cardiff, 1995) Vernon Higham helpfully expounded Isaiah 62 to 64 in the context of revival.

The plea of chapter 64 must be referring to events beyond the days of Hezekiah and therefore represents a longing for God to do again what he did in the time of that king. Isaiah lived on into the time of Hezekiah's son, Manasseh, whose reign of wickedness continued for half a century until most of his father's achievements had been reversed. Clearly the prophet is speaking against the background of a ruined city of Jerusalem (vv. 10–11). But there was no wholesale destruction of Jerusalem until the time of Nebuchadnezzar of Babylon in 587 BC—one hundred and seventy years after Isaiah began his ministry. Therefore, Isaiah is looking forward prophetically to something he himself will never live to see. But in declaring the destruction of the cities across Judah, including the city of Jerusalem itself and, most terrible of all, the temple (vv. 10–11), he is also aware of the restoration of the city.

In his mind, the prophet moves beyond the restoration of the city and temple in the time of Ezra and Nehemiah to the creation of 'new heavens and a new earth' (65:17). From this point on, the whole picture is beyond earthly Zion and passes to and through the gospel age into the final act of God in history.

Calvin sees this reference to the new heavens and new earth as 'exaggerated modes of expression to refer to the gospel age of the coming Messiah.' But he continues, 'Nor does he mean only the first coming, but the whole reign, which must be extended as far as to the last coming'.[61] On the well-known passage of the wolf and the lamb (65:25 cf. 11:6–9) Calvin concludes, 'Beyond all controversy the Prophet speaks allegorically of bloody and violent men, whose cruel and savage nature shall be subdued, when they submit to the yoke of Christ.'[62] E. J. Young says much the same thing, 'In the concept of the prophet, time and eternity, the age of the New Testament and the eternal heaven, are not sharply distinguished.'[63]

61 Calvin on Isaiah, (Baker, 1979), p. 398.
62 Calvin, p. 406.
63 E. J. Young, *The Book of Isaiah* (Eerdmans, 1972), p. 514.

In the light of this, what do we expect when we follow this passage as a pattern-prayer for revival? Before we answer that, we should look at the verses themselves.

63:15–19. The ground upon which Isaiah takes his stand is that God sees all and must surely be concerned for the state of those who carry his honour in this world. The plea is based upon God's will ('your zeal'), his emotions ('your tenderness and compassion'), and his relationship with his people ('you are our Father ... our Redeemer'). Boldly, the prophet accuses God of inaction, as a result of which his servants have been hardened and have become indistinguishable from those who have never been God's special people. There is a daring courage about the way the prophet addresses God in his prayer, which would be arrogant presumption if it did not come from a man who had been through the humbling experience of chapter 6. It is a prayer that challenges God to act.

64:1–3. Isaiah is pleading for a miracle. This is evident from his poetry. Mixing his metaphors, he longs for an awesome revelation of divine power that would be like shaking mountains (as God did on Sinai) as easily as fire burns brushwood or boils water. Such an intervention would make both the name and presence of God known and revered among the nations.

64:4–7. The prophet has no doubt where the fault lies. Jerusalem's God is the only true God and he is always ready to help those who rely on him, find their joy in him and who walk in righteousness. But God has good reason to be angry with his people, who continue to walk in their sinful disobedience. Isaiah confesses that he and the people are like filthy rags and are tossed about like a dead leaf in the wind; no one cries out to God or clings desperately to him. Their perilous state is all that they deserve.

64:8–12. The only claim that Isaiah can make upon God is that he represents the people whom God adopted and moulded for his use. Tragically, this claim appears incongruous in the light of the state of the city of Jerusalem—a desolate wilderness. All that was good is now ruined. In the light of this how can God hold back from coming to help his people?

In the chapter that follows God adds to the desperate picture by underscoring their sin which was their only response to his grace. But in promising better times ahead, it is not for the present generation, who have neglected God's repeated plea to return to him, but for their descendants (65:9–10). The fact that the prophecy is looking forward to the coming of the Messiah is clear from verses 13–16 and the reference to a people called 'by another name'. From here Isaiah moved immediately into the promise of 'new heavens and a new earth' (vv. 17–25).

How can we use chapter 64 as a prayer for revival? That is exactly what Isaiah was longing for. The cause and ground of his prayer is precisely the same for the church today. The answer to Isaiah's prayer lay in the future of the age of the Messiah, but that does not alter the significance of the prayer. We are longing, like Isaiah, for God to respond with such a supernatural intervention that the whole world will be shaken as fire burns brushwood and boils water. He did this with the coming of the Messiah. Paul applied 64:4 to the time of the gospel (1 Corinthians 2:9).

There is no specific promise of revival for us in this whole passage, but we can certainly use Isaiah's anguish and longing in our own prayer.

JEREMIAH 14:7–9, 19–22—A PEOPLE DECEIVED BY PROMISES OF PEACE AND PROSPERITY

Jeremiah's ministry covered almost half a century from 626 BC to the fall of Jerusalem in 587 BC and beyond. He preached through the reigns of five kings in Judah, from Josiah to Zedekiah. Brought up in a priestly home, Jeremiah was called to his ministry as a young man at the beginning of the reforms of Josiah. In fact, Jeremiah's early preaching probably significantly contributed to Josiah's zeal, together with the rediscovery of the law of God.

With the untimely death of Josiah in battle, Jeremiah found himself among a backsliding people who were ripe for judgement. Frequently he stood alone, warning of judgement whilst the false prophets assured the nation that all would be well. He suffered severely for this, particularly during the time of the Babylonian siege of Jerusalem. Although Jeremiah was an uncompromising preacher of judgement, he was also the prophet who assured the nation that their suffering and exile would not last for ever, and that a return and restoration would follow.

The prophecies recorded in Jeremiah are not all in chronological order, though it is most likely that this passage belongs to the time of Josiah. Manasseh and his son Amon had left the nation in a terrible state. The half century of Manasseh's evil reign was hardly improved even after his repentance at the close of his life, and Amon continued the same spiritual slide. Josiah came to the throne at the age of eight, and at the age of sixteen he set himself to seek the Lord. In the twelfth year of his reign the king began his reforms (2 Chronicles 34:1–3).

Significantly it was a year later that Jeremiah commenced his own ministry (Jeremiah 1:1–2) although it was not until another five years had passed that the law was rediscovered in the temple (2 Chronicles 34:14). Jeremiah 14:19–22 must be seen, not in the light of Josiah's early reforms, but in the light of the many decades of decadence that preceded Josiah. Reform is not the same as revival and Jeremiah's great complaint was that there appeared to be little change of heart among the people. They were content simply to do the right things.

14:7–9. The people were suffering a period of severe drought as a punishment for their 'backslidings'; the prophet's plea is a cry for rain. He acknowledged the nation's sin and his bitter regret was the paradox that although the Lord was 'among us', he appeared to be nothing more than a passing traveller in the land; unknown even to his own people. The desperate plea, 'Do not forsake us!', came from a man who knew the bitter consequences of God walking away from his own people. God responded by saying that since they have wandered from him, he would no longer listen to them or take notice of their empty ritual (vv. 10–12). Unfortunately, Jeremiah was not the only preacher in his day; others were holding out the promise of peace and prosperity that led the people into a false security that all was well. They could point to the current reforms of Josiah as evidence of that.

14:19–20. The warning of 'sword and famine' led Jeremiah to pour out one of his most powerful prayers on record. He has a cluster of strong words to describe how he believes the people have been treated by God: rejected, despised, afflicted, dishonoured. Contrary to the promises of the false prophets, there was no healing, no peace, nothing agreeable. But the prophet turned these descriptions into questions because they appeared to be inconsistent with all the promises of God: 'Have you?' 'Why have you?' However, Jeremiah knew only too well that whilst God's ultimate promise to his people was unconditional, it did not mean that they would not be punished for bad behaviour (see for example 2 Samuel 7:13–16). Therefore, without waiting for an answer, Jeremiah confessed their 'wickedness, guilt and sin'.

It is wildly dangerous to tolerate sloppy and sinful activity by placing our confidence in 'evidence' that God is with us.

> It is wildly dangerous to tolerate sloppy and sinful activity by placing our confidence in 'evidence' that God is with us

14:21–22. Then followed the only claim the prophet could make upon God. There were no excuses, only a hope that God would act for his own sake, that he would recognize that in the disgrace of his people was his own disgrace and that he had a covenant commitment to the people. Besides, where else could the prophet go? None of the idols of the surrounding nations could produce rain. God alone was their LORD and God. In the light of all this, Jeremiah was determined to 'hope' for God—a word that means to look eagerly and expectantly for something.

Although Jeremiah was pleading for rain, it was not rain above all that we wanted. He recognized that the real need was far bigger than this.

The absence of rain was the result of their persistent disobedience by listening to the false prophets and relying upon their daily worship ritual. Only a spiritual revival could turn the hand of God for them instead of against them.

Once again, we have a prayer that must be understood before it is used. There are close applications to be made to the life of our churches today and it may be painful to turn the finger of God through Jeremiah against ourselves—but it must be done. The parallels may be obvious with a moment of thought. God will no more respond to the self-satisfaction of his people today than he did then. Whatever our equivalent of 'rain', we should learn from the prophet that is not our greatest need.

DANIEL 9:4-19—A MODEL PRAYER FOR REVIVAL

The unbroken succession of the prophets continues. Daniel was a teenager when he was taken into exile in Babylon around the year 587 BC. As Jeremiah came to the close of his ministry, Daniel was at the threshold of his own. As with Jeremiah, the book of Daniel is not in strict chronological order, but by the time of this prayer, Daniel was an old man of around eighty years who had maintained his integrity of life and faith under six pagan and repressive rulers.

In his regular, daily time of prayer, he had been reading in the prophet Jeremiah. Sadly, many of the sins that caused the people to be taken into exile had stayed with them, and in Daniel's prayer we can hear the same urgent cry that we have found in Hosea, Isaiah and Jeremiah. Daniel, like all the prophets, prayed in the first-person plural 'we'. It is identification with the people. In preaching the prophets speak on behalf of God to the people and therefore they point the finger and condemn the sins. In praying, they do not pray 'for them' but 'for us'—'we have sinned'. They identify themselves with the sins of those who bear the name of the LORD.

Verse 2. His prayer was based on the promises of God—Jeremiah 29:10–14...

Verses 4, 7, 8. ...and on the character of God—great, awesome, covenant of love, righteous, merciful, forgiving.

Verses 5–7. His confession was focused—sin, iniquity, wickedness, rebellion, disobedience, unfaithfulness.

Verses 7–8. And the results were understood—shame and disgrace.

Verses 11–14. Daniel accepted that the punishment was just—as Moses warned and because the LORD is righteous.

> In praying, the prophets do not pray 'for them' but 'for us'—'we have sinned'. They identify themselves with the sins of those who bear the name of the LORD

Verse 12. The disaster is great—there had been nothing like it before.

Verse 16. But there is a covenant claim—we are a special people.

Verses 17–19. More particularly the honour of God is at stake—'for your sake' and the sake of your name.

Verses 17–19. There is a bold urgency—'Hear our prayers', 'look at the desolation of your city', 'forgive', 'don't delay'.

More than half a century earlier, God looked for someone to stand before him in prayer on behalf of the nation (Ezekiel 22:30). He found no one, so the judgement fell. Daniel was a teenager then, but he is now determined to stand in the gap. Did God hear and respond? The answer is found in 2 Chronicles 36:22–23.

This courageous, daring and insistent prayer is available for God's people in every age of the church to use—providing they have the same repentant heart and God-honouring purpose as Daniel.

PSALM 44—DISHONOUR WHEN WE HAVE TRIED TO BE FAITHFUL

Here is a very different cause for prayer. Could this be more appropriate for the believing church today than any other passage we are considering? A people who humbly believe that they have done all they can to please

God yet discover that there is still no sign that God is with them. Hosea, Isaiah, Jeremiah and Daniel, identified the sins that were the cause of the nation's spiritual ill health and the consequent dishonour to God. However, sometimes we are mystified at our apparent neglect by God. It is not that we claim

> Sometimes we are mystified at our apparent neglect by God

to be perfect, but we have sincerely tried to please him in every way.

A summary of the psalm reveals the writer's perplexity: You have helped us in the past; we still boast about you helping us; but you are not helping us now; therefore, you must help us.

We do not know who wrote this psalm or on what occasion. It forms a trio with Psalms 42 and 43 where the psalmist longs for God in his discouragement and yearns for the time when he can yet again worship at Jerusalem. The references in Psalm 44 to being scattered among the nations (v. 11) and the mocking derision of the nations (v. 14) would indicate some time in the exile; this would make it contemporaneous with Daniel.[64] If this is so, we have discovered another small group of faithful Jews in the land of exile. The title 'of the sons of Korah' would imply that singing was one way the exiles encouraged each other, because the descendants of Korah were the temple musicians. What is without a doubt is the theme.

THE PSALMIST'S PROMISE OF LOYALTY:

Verses 1–3. Singing was not the only way that the faithful encouraged each other. They read the stories of God's great deliverance in the past, and in doing so acknowledged that victory did not belong to the nation, but to God alone. Clearly the psalmist, and those he represents, found

---

64 Leupold puts it in the time of David (900 BC), though even Spurgeon is not sure about this, and Calvin places it in the time of the Maccabees (150 BC). So, who knows?

great delight in reading the history of God's dealing with his people and admired the times when the people were faithful.

Verses 4–8. But the psalmist insisted that it was no different with him and his people. They also sincerely claimed God to be their King and they would not trust in themselves. They constantly boasted that God alone was their hope and all their trust was in him. In the past they had proved this, and they were still not ashamed to claim it—despite all appearances to the contrary.

Verse 17. They had not forgotten God and they had tried to live as his covenant people should live. They had kept their heart intent on pleasing him and had walked according to his word.

Verses 20–21. If all this is hypocrisy and a sham, God would know because no secret can be hidden from him.

THE PSALMIST'S PROTEST OF NEGLECT:

Verses 9–12. You appear to have abandoned us; all our best efforts to serve you come to nothing. We achieve little, and often go backward instead of forward. You gain nothing by our lack of success, but still you do not take action to help us.

Verses 13–16, 19, 22. Those around us laugh and despise us. The world shakes its head in pity. They see us as yesterday's men and women. We cannot escape their constant mocking, and instead of us spoiling the world, the world spoils us. Every day we are like food for jackals and sheep for slaughter.

THE PSALMIST'S PRAYER FOR HELP:

Verses 23–24. Can it be that you are asleep to our desperate need? Have you cast us away from your love for ever? Why do you hide your face from us? Why do you forget your own people in their affliction?

Verse 25. We can hardly go any lower than we are.

Verse 26. It is time to stir yourself so that people will honour you as a God of mercy.

The boldness of the psalmist here is staggering. He dares to suggest to God: 'We have not forgotten you, but you appear to have forgotten us; we talk of you all day long, but you seem to be asleep.' To offer such a prayer is arrogant presumption unless we are certain that God himself would approve of the claim we make about ourselves. God wants his people to be bold with him, but never presumptuous and never arrogant. Certainly, we can pray as the psalmist prayed, but only when our promise of loyalty is as convincing as his. Let that be true, and this psalm is ours to pray.

PSALM 77—I CANNOT ALLOW MYSELF TO BE DISCOURAGED

The theme of this psalm is not too dissimilar from Psalm 44 except that was a corporate psalm—the 'we' and 'us' were predominant—whereas this one is intensely personal. The psalmist is alone with his problem. It is a model of the way in which we may counsel ourselves when we are discouraged. How to lift ourselves up when we are cast down is a lost art among many Christians today; we prefer to run to the counsellor instead—or remain despondent.

We are told who wrote this psalm. Asaph was chief choirmaster under King David and his instrument was the cymbals (1 Chronicles 16:4–5). Two hundred years later Asaph's psalms, and those of David, formed the songbook of revival in the time of Hezekiah (2 Chronicles 29:30). What was the cause of his despair we do not know, but it is commonplace for Christians today to feel overwhelmed by the hardness of people's hearts and their strong opposition to the gospel. When our best efforts come to nothing, and at times even God himself seems to be a long way off, there is always the temptation to give up. Asaph has left us a wise example.

Verse 1. Before he plunges into despair, our psalmist establishes at least this much: 'I cried out to God for help; I cried out to God to hear me.' If all else seemed to be against him, that much he would persist in. It was his one firm constant. There was nowhere else to turn.

Verses 2–3. Such was his despair that it seemed as if his very soul refused to accept comfort, and even thinking about God and calling out to him made his circumstances all the more inexplicable. But he was certain of this: he would go to God with his complaining, and to no one else.

Verses 4–6. The psalmist could not sleep, so he allowed his mind to be distracted from its present anxiety by thinking of past blessings from God. Diligently he ransacked the story of God's providence to himself to remind himself of the interventions of God.

Verses 7–9. Unfortunately, that had the opposite effect of his intentions! It appeared that:

> God no longer did what he used to do;
> his once gracious mercy had now ceased;
> his promises had run dry and had failed;
> he had even forgotten to be gracious ever again;
> he was relentlessly angry.

Verses 10–15. Nevertheless—and here is the psalmist's secret—he will persist not only in recalling God's great deeds in the past but will also think about them and talk about them. In that way he will encourage others and be encouraged himself. He will become more and more convinced of the reality of God's mercy, the necessity of his mercy and the possibility of his mercy.

Verses 16–20. He seems not to have progressed beyond Moses in his recollection of history. The parting of the great rivers and the awesome events of Sinai were enough to convince him that although God's footprints are not always seen, they are always there; and that although Moses and Aaron may not always have made a good job of their leadership God was, after all, the great Shepherd.

The psalm ends at this point. Perhaps he had resolved his problem by now and was settled in the conviction that the absence of God was more apparent than real; and that all the negatives that seemed so real would evaporate in the light of true reality.

Spurgeon comments on this psalm: 'It has much sadness in it, but we may be sure it will end well, for it begins with prayer, and prayer never has an ill issue.' It is true that reflecting on the past great deeds of God may at times only compound our confusion, but that is no bad thing if it drives us more fervently to God. We seem to be so far from the possibility of God changing the condition of our churches and our society, and what God has done in the past is hard to imagine for our present circumstances. In fact, he does not seem to act in that way anymore.

These thoughts can easily depress us unless we learn from Asaph. Far from abandoning his reading of the history of salvation, it only compelled him to look closer and deeper into the story of God's great activity for his people. As he did so, his heart became more convinced that God is God alone and all hope belongs to him. Once begun, Asaph continued his reading, and Psalm 78 expands the theme. If we long for revival in our day, we must never allow a generation to grow up in ignorance of the footprints of God.

PSALM 85—AGAIN, LORD!

This psalm is different again. Unlike Psalms 44 or 77, the psalmist seems to have lived through a time of revival and he therefore knows from personal experience what that means. It is another psalm from the descendants of Korah. Since there is a reference to the LORD having brought his people back from captivity (v. 1) we could place it during the time of Ezra-Nehemiah

> If we long for revival in our day, we must never allow a generation to grow up in ignorance of the footprints of God

when, after the decree of Cyrus, the early zeal of the return had settled to a cold routine. But this is not certain. Spurgeon, typically, adamantly attributes it to David; at a time when the land was oppressed by the Philistines. Leupold suggests shortly after the return from the Babylonian captivity. Calvin, with no compelling reason, believes it was composed 'to be sung by the people when they were persecuted by the cruel tyranny of Antiochus'—presumably he meant Antiochus IV which would place it a little earlier than his suggestion for Psalm 44. Leupold is the most probable. The prophets Haggai and Zechariah were sent to challenge the returned exiles to a new zeal and perhaps this lament was composed at the same time; evidently singing was a significant part of the people's worship (Nehemiah 12:45–47).

Verses 1–3. The LORD 'showed favour', 'restored the fortunes', 'forgave the iniquity', 'set aside all your wrath' and more. If this took place at the return from exile, our psalmist was there. The people's response at that time is recorded in Ezra 3.

Verses 4–7. Clearly the spiritual life of the nation is flagging. The psalmist plays on the same word that he has used of God in verse 3, as God *turned* from the fierceness of his anger so they need to be *restored* to him (it is the same word). With good reason God has turned away from them. This could have been when the people did not persist in their efforts to rebuild the temple (Ezra 4) or later when Nehemiah drew attention to necessary reforms (Nehemiah 13). The consequence of their disobedience was that their joy in God and their experience of salvation had evaporated.

The psalmist presents God with a choice: Will you (repeated) be angry for ever, or will you revive us? The word used here means 'quicken, refresh, restore, revive'. It has to do with new life. He longs for their joy to be restored as the people are revived. The Puritan Thomas Watson wrote, 'God has no design upon us, but to make us happy', and Spurgeon comments on verse 6, 'God loves to see his children happy.' But each meant happiness found in God. Revival is one of the best ways by which God can make his people happy. Joy is a hallmark of revival.

Verses 8–9. The fearful questions in verse 5 were clearly rhetorical since the psalmist is confident of the outcome: he will again hear the Lord speaking peace to the people. However, it can quickly be lost if they do not firmly resist the temptation to slide back into folly. The psalmist has a clear priority in his mind. 'Glory' is the presence of God known and felt among the people. That is not only for their enjoyment, but also for God's honour.

Verses 10–13. Here is the final blend of the past and the future. In the past, when the nation followed God, both love and faithfulness met each other, and righteousness and peace kissed. God's love and faithfulness will always accompany righteousness and peace. But here, the righteousness is from heaven—it is the Lord giving what is good in response to truth springing up from the earth to meet him. The good that he will give to his people and do for them (righteousness) will go ahead of them and, unlike the psalmist in Psalm 77, they will see his footsteps clearly and will make that their pathway.

9. Encouraging prayer for revival using eyewitness accounts

Cameos of revivals

To encourage prayer for revival, it is a powerful incentive to read accounts of what God has done throughout the history of the Christian church. This is what our psalmist did in Psalm 77. In the Introduction of *Revival—a people saturated with God* a brief description was given of four occasions when God came in power among his people. They ranged from Wales, North Carolina, Malawi and Scotland and from 1743 to 1949. It would take only a few minutes to read them all to a prayer meeting.

What follows is a selection of cameos each of which would take only a few minutes to read. These are taken from eyewitness accounts and carry that authentic 'feel' from someone who could say, 'I was there.'

Chapter 9

....

I was there: Bulford, Wiltshire 1860–61

BULFORD CONGREGATIONAL CHURCH

The following is compiled from the account taken in September 1980 by Peter Beale, the then pastor of the church, from the Church Book of the Independent Chapel at Bulford, Wiltshire. John Protheroe trained at the Independent Academy in Newport Pagnell College which was founded by William Bull in 1782. Protheroe was called as pastor at Bulford in August 1840. After seven years he resigned the pastorate, partly because of his poor health and partly for what he considered to be 'a want of success' in his ministry. After six years in Plymouth he was recalled to Bulford in 1853 but initially there was only slow growth, with just five members added during the first six years. During the two years of revival the membership increased by fifty-three. The events are recorded in the Church Book dated March 1861 by John Protheroe himself.

For some time, a few of the most spiritual in the membership were convinced that God was about to come to the church in mercy. They were not disappointed. 'The first indications of the great work became visible about the end of November last (1860) and were observed in the quiet stillness which pervaded the Congregation.' There was an earnest desire to see a general awakening and this was accompanied by 'the extraordinary spirit of prayer which was poured out upon the people, and their faith in the efficacy of prayer.' At the same time, the pastor felt a 'mysterious and almost irresistible' conviction regarding the subjects he must preach on and was aware of the Holy Spirit's aid in preaching.

In the second week of 1860 the church spent a week 'on its knees in prayer to God ... For some few months after that event we had meetings for prayer, almost every night in the week. These meetings were never forgotten.' There were other meetings for prayer and fellowship and as a result, 'Duty became a pleasure, and the preaching of the Cross—always a favourite work—now became doubly so to me.'

It became evident during the revival that many had been challenged and awakened even before the revival began: 'From the conversation I have had with inquirers after salvation and candidates for church fellowship, it appears that, in the generality of cases, there had been a deep impression produced under the ministry of the Word sometime before any immediate indications of a revival were seen; and I learn that under one sermon preached by me, from the words, "Whosoever shall be ashamed of me", at least nine months before the awakening actually took place, five or six persons were deeply and savingly impressed, and led to the Cross and to the throne. A similar remark may be made with regard to other sermons preached about that time.'

The revival meant that the membership of the church almost trebled and at one church meeting twenty new members were announced with another ten as candidates. 'The awakening at Bulford has been very general—among young and old—among persons of every character, who have displayed a firm determination to become personally interested in the privileges and blessings of the kingdom of heaven, and an ardent desire to become recognized subjects of it.'

'For the last four months, meetings for prayer have been held almost every night in the week, and are generally crowded. The effects of the present awakening on our young people are remarkable; they pray not only for themselves, but for their relatives and friends and the unconverted in the village and neighbourhood with great earnestness. It is astonishing to what a wonderful degree they are blessed with the gift of prayer. There is no loss for words, no hesitation as generally is the case with young converts when they begin to pray. Their language flows, apparently without any let or hinderance. Some of these young converts are not more than sixteen years of age. Praise to God for what he has done for their souls, and an appeal to his throne to accomplish for their relatives and neighbours what he has done for them, form a principal part of their prayer … And then, having dwelt upon other subjects, they usually conclude with fervent and affectionate prayer for their minister and for those friends whom they designate the "Supporters" of the Cause at Bulford.

'Even little children now pray—they are not passed by … Indeed, all pray—old and young. They cannot but pray; they are filled with the Spirit of prayer; and consequently they pray with an unction and a readiness and frequency and earnestness which must strike with astonishment all who hear them. And when on the Sabbath or on week evenings the regular service is over—a service perhaps of more than two hours' duration, and sometimes three—a great number of them linger about, as if unwilling to leave, and then return to pray, and continue till late supplicating God's throne for the conversion of ungodly relatives and friends, or that of the whole village.

'Those of them to whom formerly the language of prayer was a stranger, and who, on religious subjects, appeared as if they were possessed with a dumb spirit, now express their thoughts before the throne with a readiness and fluency which is truly astonishing. For some years past a prayer meeting has been held in the schoolroom adjoining the chapel on the Sabbath evening immediately before the service. The place is now generally crowded, there is only standing room there. And the early Sabbath prayer meeting held at 7 o'clock in the morning is now well attended.

'At the week-evening prayer meetings, which are held almost every night in the week, I always speak for about 20 minutes or half an hour either from a single verse or a larger portion of God's Word; and, having finished, I express my wish that two or three of the brethren—without specifying their names—would pray successively without singing between, and then another hymn is sung and five or six more pray as before; nine or ten usually pray at these meetings; though one night as many as sixteen engaged in prayer.

'I have seldom had a meeting without having at its close some inquirers after salvation. One night as many as fifteen persons remained after the service to converse with me about the concerns of their souls. For these inquirers, for the young converts and for the members generally, I have established a weekly meeting for reading together the Word of God, for mutual conversation and spiritual edification and encouragement—a meeting at which we have felt the presence of the Master, and we have exclaimed, "It is good for us to be here."

'A large proportion of the Candidates for Church fellowship are found among the young; some few of whom, before their conversion and while in the Sabbath School, were almost unmanageable by their teachers. Now they are in their right mind and pray. It is a pleasure to hear these young converts in their prayers refer with gratitude to the early impressions made upon their minds when they were taught in the School; and with hearts overflowing with joy, not only acknowledging this but praying most fervently and affectionately for their former teachers.

'The present revival at Bulford is distinguished more by deep inward solemnity than by any external manifestation: there is no physical prostration, no outward extravagance, no religious bustle. There has been no approach whatever to anything like it; nor am I aware of anything specially remarkable, in this respect. However, there is the case of one young man who commented that one Sabbath morning, while he was listening to me preaching from the words: "I will hear what God the Lord will speak, for he will speak unto his people and to the saints; but let them not turn again to folly", he felt as if he must fall off his seat; his sins appearing to him in all their magnitude, and malignity and number.

'For the rest, there is a deep sense of their previous guilty and perilous condition as sinners, and an impression that they may at any time unexpectedly be called out of the world, together with strong faith in the efficacy of prayer. Among some of the principal characteristics by which the converts, whether young or old, are distinguished are a calm and happy frame of mind and a consistent walk.'

'A happy change has come over the Village, and everywhere around the influence [of the revival] is felt. The Police-Officer, located in our neighbourhood, referring to this happy change, one day remarked that, in his walks thro' Bulford, instead of trifling conversation he could now hear only the voice of prayer and praise ascending to God, from the cottages of the poor which may now be styled "Bethels". And the young people instead of frequenting as formerly they did the public houses, now abstain altogether from intoxicating drinks and derive their chief delight from the service of God. The fields, too, present a very different aspect from what they ever had before. Here and there, during the dinner hour you may see and hear groups of persons while resting speaking of the things touching the King, and, perhaps, one of their number reading to the rest some religious book. Oh, what hath God wrought!'

John Protheroe concluded that two things struck him forcibly in the time of revival. The first was 'The necessity of Divine influence and the vast importance of depending more and more upon the promised aid of the Spirit in the discharge of all religious duties.' The second was the importance and power of prayer: 'We had long been praying for this revival—crying long, but believingly and patiently, "from beneath the altar". It is now come. The Lord has come into His Temple. He blesses his people with peace. The voice had long been heard crying in the wilderness, Prepare ye the way of the Lord. And now in the wilderness—in a desert— the desert of the heart—a highway for our God has been made straight, while many a heart has lifted up its gate for the King of glory to come in.'

I was there: Rhosllanerchrugog (Rhos), North Wales 1904

THE WELSH BAPTIST CHAPEL (PENUEL)

John Powell Parry was born in 1887 and was therefore seventeen years of age in 1904 when the revival came to Rhosllanerchrugog, a mining town three miles south of Wrexham in North Wales. This account is taken from a recorded interview by Paul Cook of Hull with Powell Parry on 2 October 1974 in Plas Bennion, a small hamlet near Ruabon just south of Rhos. Powell Parry died on 27 June 1979 at the age of ninety-two.

In 1904 Rhosllanerchrugog was a Welsh-speaking mining town, with few English people living there. Almost every man worked down the pits and Powell Parry himself was working underground by the age of fourteen. Wages were poor and life was hard, the boys working a nine-and-a-half hours shift for three shillings (fifteen pence) a day; there was little social concern for the condition of the people and drink was a widespread social evil.

In spite of this, there was great respect for the Bible and ministers, so much so that the Bible was a subject of discussion even in the public houses. There were many preachers in the town who, though not well educated or men with degrees, nevertheless took their call to the ministry seriously; they stood firmly on the authority of Scripture, and 'modernism' was unknown among them. Churches and chapels were full and Sunday morning services were packed. The Christians were a serious people and whilst not expecting revival, they were concerned that the doctrine of the churches was pure. In the chapels two discerning elders would sit in the 'big pew', beneath the pulpit and facing the congregation, to discern any error in the preaching. Discipline and holy living were expected of the members and the town knew this; Christians were noticeably different and were generally respected.

The revival in Rhos started quite unexpectedly in the Welsh Baptist Chapel where Rhys Bevan Jones, from South Wales, had been invited to conduct a mission. The first knowledge that Powell Parry had about the revival came as he returned home early one morning at the close of the night shift. A young man told him that something wonderful was happening at Penuel Chapel, and as Powell came near to the church it was evident that something remarkable was going on: 'People were rejoicing, and it was bursting out of the walls and into the streets.'

Revival spread rapidly through the whole town until every church was affected. The Methodists, Congregationalists, Salvation Army, the Church of England and Baptists were all caught up in the great wave of revival so that 'denominationalism disappeared' and you could enter any church in the town and find crowds of people at prayer; there was a great harmony in the town.

This was a revival of praise and thanksgiving in which people learnt to enjoy God. There was a life and reality about everything that was done in the churches; people were involved with eternal issues and 'things' didn't seem to matter anymore. In the Baptist Chapel R. B. Jones would sit at the front in the 'big pew' with his open Bible. He ensured that nothing took place contrary to Scripture. He preached every night from 8 to 18 November. Services ran without an order, but there was no confusion either; people would sing and pray and praise as the Spirit led them. Rhys Jones made sure that things never got out of hand, and in all the enthusiasm and joy, Powell Parry noted that there was never any excess in the town. 'No one ever spoke of tongues or a second blessing; it was all peace and quiet and tranquility.' It was very unlike some of the events that accompanied the revival that was going on in other parts of Wales at the same time, under Evan Roberts.

On Sundays the chapels were full by six in the morning. The pits worked an eleven-day fortnight and every other Monday was an extra day off; this was known as the 'playing Monday'; in the revival the 'playing Monday' was given over entirely to worship.

Crowds could be heard simply walking along the streets singing and praising God, and when most of the Rhos silver band were converted they took to playing hymns in the open air. Mothers would be up at dawn, and when their husbands left for work they completed the housework early, saw the children off to school and then went to the chapel to worship. This was happening all over the town. Yet though the men spent hours in the chapels after a full day of work, no one appeared to be tired; 'there was life in the air' and people seemed to be physically as well as spiritually revived.

The effect of the revival on the unconverted was amazing. Hundreds were saved and it seemed as though the whole town was coming to church. People gave up drinking and smoking, and tobacco pouches and pipes were placed on the 'big pew' as a mark of the changed life. 'The terror of the Lord had fallen on the whole town', and within a few weeks many drunkards were afraid to come out of their homes or go into the public houses, which were being forced to close throughout 1905 because of a lack of customers. The famous football team, the Rhos Rangers, were afraid to go out and play; in fact, for a while the club closed because there were no spectators.

Fighting was a popular sport before the revival and William Price, a well-known fighter in the town, was converted. He had never been to chapel before, and after his conversion he was so full of joy that he reproached the Christians by asking, 'Why didn't you tell me, my friends, that it was like this?' Another fighter, Levi Jarvis, was the terror of the town. He was opposed to the work of God but at the same time was terrified of it. The terror had become terrified. He was afraid to go to work, and once there, was afraid to come home again in case he got converted. He could not sleep at night, and he went off his food. Levi Jarvis knew that people were praying for him and this only made him more afraid; his wife feared that he would go out of his mind. One day Rhys Jones came to visit the home to reassure Levi's wife that they were praying. When Jarvis learnt of this he swallowed his meal and fled to the mountains to get away from the revival. But God eventually saved him and the congregation watched the great fighter raise his hands in the air as a mark of his surrender to the Lord. Levi Jarvis the fighter became like a lamb. He was in his forties when he was saved and he had turned eighty when he died, but he never went back on his surrender to Christ. Powell knew him well and talked with him in his old age; Levi would often invite him with the words: 'Come on, let's talk about the revival.'

Life changed in the pits also, and men would meet for prayer before the day's work commenced. 'The Spirit was in the pits … It was as pleasant to go to work as it was to go to a place of worship.' There was no tension or disputes among the miners, and output was one hundred per cent. Everyone was talking about being saved, and men were even saved down the mines. Even those who were not saved were deeply affected.

Ponies were used to haul the coal trucks at that time, and two men were employed to look after them. There could be as many as ninety or more ponies in one pit, and it was long and hard work caring for the harness and feeding and grooming the ponies. After the revival came, a foreman found the man in charge of the ponies in a terrible state of mind, afraid that he would lose his job: the boys were each looking after his own pony and there was nothing for the man to do.

As the news of the revival spread, people travelled from all over Wales to see what was happening. Then they came from other parts of Britain and from the United States, Canada, Australia and elsewhere. Many of these visitors carried the revival away with them to distant parts of the world. Such was the presence of God that it could be felt by visitors as soon as they entered the town, and even beyond this. Powell Parry comments, 'The presence of God was everywhere.'

As an example of this awareness of the presence of God, he recalls the story of an event during the summer of 1905, when a Christian man arrived in Rhos with his two daughters from Barrow-in-Furness, in north-west Lancashire. He came to the 'big pew' in the Baptist Chapel and told his experience to the congregation—which included the teenage Powell Parry. This Lancastrian had read of the revival in his daily paper and one of his daughters had suggested they might go and visit the town to see for themselves what was happening. They caught the Sunday midnight slow train and arrived in Chester station at 6.00 a.m. Not knowing where to go from here, they enquired of a porter: 'How do we get to the place where the revival is?' They were told there would be a train at 8.00 a.m. to Wrexham and from there they could catch a local train to Rhos. 'But how will we know when we are near Wrexham?', they asked. 'Oh', replied the porter, 'You'll feel it in the train.' And they did! There was an unmistakable expectancy in the air. Two miles outside Rhos they enquired again and were told, 'Go down that road and you will feel it down there.' It was 9.00 a.m. on a 'playing Monday' when the visitor and his two daughters arrived at the chapel to find it already full of worshippers who had been there since 7.00 a.m.

There were no special meetings for young people; they all came to the adult meetings. Even children of six and eight years of age were talking about Jesus, even though they were not all converted, and teachers would weep as they overheard the children's conversations.

The effects of this revival continued right up until the Great War in 1914. Prayer meetings were changed and revitalized, and the 'experience meeting', where the Christians shared their testimony of God's goodness, proved a means of grace to many.

Powell Parry identified a number of factors that began to quench the work of the Spirit following the war. Modernism came into the pulpits as 'educated' men came from the colleges infected with a critical view of the Bible. A new generation, back from the war, wanted this 'modern preaching'. Powell said plainly of one such minister: 'He was a dud!' Modernism took the pulpit and emptied the chapels. At the same time social reform in the guise of 'practical Christianity', with its motto, 'Lift up the bottom dog, down with the idle rich,' took the spiritual life out of the churches. And, sadly, the Christians did not realize what was happening. In Powell's view, following the Second World War Welsh Nationalism sealed the death of the revival.

But for those who experienced this great outpouring of the Spirit—and revivals do not often survive beyond one generation—there is a real sense in which revival is never lost. John Powell Parry could claim seventy years later, at the age of eighty-six: 'I still have it now.'

I was there: Lowestoft (Suffolk) 1921

LONDON ROAD BAPTIST CHURCH

The following account is drawn from an interview with pastor Robert Browne on 22 March 1989 in Trowbridge. It is followed by additional comments given in Lowestoft on 30 March 1989 from Henry Hannant, who was born in 1901 and was a member of the church at the time of the revival. Robert Browne, as a boy of fifteen years, was converted on the first evening of the revival in Lowestoft, Suffolk, in 1921.[65]

This remarkable work of God commenced in the London Road Baptist Church, where the pastor, Hugh Fergusson, had invited the Rev. Douglas Brown from Balham in London to conduct a week of mission meetings. Concerned at the lack of conversions, Hugh Fergusson had called the church to prayer and for six months around sixty members met every Monday evening to pray only for revival. The effects of the revival spread throughout East Anglia and moved north to Great Yarmouth, where many of the Scottish fishermen carried the fire to their home fishing ports around Scotland. Douglas Brown had come into a new experience of God in February 1921 and on the last Sunday evening of that month ninety-six people came to faith in Christ in his London church. This account is the experience of one boy in Lowestoft.

Robert Browne was born in 1905 and was brought up to attend the Congregational Church at Oulton Broad where his parents were members. At the age of fourteen he left the Congregational Church and, though not a Christian, joined a Bible class at the London Road Baptist Church in Lowestoft towards the end of 1920; there was a good group of young people here and the church was well attended. From October to Christmas,

---

65 For a full account of this revival see Stanley Griffin, *A Forgotten Revival* (Day One Publications, 1992 and 2000).

which was the fishing season, many fishermen from Scotland joined the congregation, partly because the minister Hugh Fergusson, was a fellow Scot. Services were typically Baptist, and the minister was decidedly evangelical. Prayer meetings were fairly well attended, and some members were obviously praying for revival, though Robert Browne did not attend the prayer meeting himself at this time.

He continues the story: 'The Sunday prior to the week's mission, the Bible Class leader had urged the boys to attend the meetings during the week to hear the Rev. Douglas Brown. My friend, Alfred, and I went on the Tuesday evening. Nothing happened on the Monday or the Tuesday. There were special prayer meetings in the mornings and Bible readings in the afternoons; we just went in the evening. At the end of the Wednesday evening Douglas Brown had been preaching to a packed church and he announced the closing hymn: "I hear thy welcome voice that calls me Lord to thee..." with the chorus: "I am coming, Lord, to thee..." I cannot recall what he had been preaching about, and there was nothing emotional or sensational, but he gave an appeal for people to come forward who were seeking Christ. Alfred and I went forward and we were conscious that people were moving from all over the large building. By the end of the hymn the aisles were full; we were taken to the schoolroom, which was soon filled up.'

'In describing the atmosphere of that meeting, I can only speak of a peculiar movement, something extraordinary. There was no noise; it was very quiet and reverent. Both myself and Alfred were counselled that night and I went home and told my parents. The next day I attended the afternoon Bible reading which, because the Baptist Church was too small for the crowds (though it could seat seven hundred), was held at Christ Church where the Rev. John Hayes was vicar. The meeting of the previous night had been "noised abroad" and hundreds were now attending. The Thursday evening meeting was back in the Baptist Church and I recall Mr Fergusson announcing, "There are so many people in the street outside wanting to get in, that I would like those of you who are Christians to leave your seats and go to the schoolroom to pray." He then walked up and down the aisles encouraging people to move to the schoolroom. Not untypically, we young people kept to our seats because we did not want to miss anything! That evening many more came to Christ.'

'Douglas Brown was booked to return to London for the weekend, and many of the young people went to the station to see him off because they had become so enthused by what was happening. But before he left, Douglas Brown promised that, in the light of what had happened, he would come back on Monday. He returned on Monday for another week of meetings, and this arrangement continued for four weeks. He admitted to having been unusually aided by God with both physical and mental strength, because he was preaching to his own congregation in London on Sunday and returning to Lowestoft for afternoon Bible readings and evening gospel meetings. The meetings moved to St John's parish church, which at that time was the largest building available in the town. It was well known to the fishermen for its tall spire that provided their landmark as they entered harbour. At this time all the evangelical churches were working together in the town, including two Anglican churches, the Baptist and the Sailors' Mission.'

'Douglas Brown was in great demand all over East Anglia, and among the many services he preached at was one held in the parish church at Oulton. There, hundreds knelt at the altar in a full commitment to Christ. Among those hundreds was myself, who, though only fifteen at the time, felt sure of my call to be a preacher. I was baptized soon afterwards, along with eighteen other young fellows, and one girl!'

'Douglas Brown preached also for the evangelical vicar in Yarmouth, and here many of the fishermen were converted. Brown was a tall, handsome man with thick white hair. His strong personality came through when he was in the pulpit and his preaching was dramatic; some even accused him of over-much acting. The great burden of his message was the need for repentance and the greatness of the Saviour. Services were alive and there was a desire among the Christians to bear witness. All over the town people would be asking each other, "Have you heard Douglas Brown?" I can recall being asked this question in Oulton by a friend of the family who was never converted and had little interest in spiritual things.'

'Like so many revivals, this great work of God in Lowestoft did not last long. It seemed to fade out, but its influence certainly remained. There would be more than 150 at the Monday prayer meeting, and many young people joined it. I can hear now a young boy often praying like an adult. Young people were winning friends to Christ and a number of them, after 1921, joined a village preaching plan. The church sent preachers to many villages around Lowestoft, and groups of young people would accompany them and give testimony; this was how many were introduced to preaching, including myself. The revival gave us a great desire to tell others the gospel. I worked in a factory at that time [1922]; it was a godless place, but I would read my Bible during the lunch breaks. After lunch on a Saturday, four or five of us would go to the Baptist church for prayer, then go to the home of one of the friends for tea and afterwards hold an open-air meeting. Every Saturday we would hold an open-air meeting somewhere in the town. We were all teenagers, fifteen and sixteen years old. We just said what we thought we would say; we had no rule or anything. I went so far as to go into a public house to preach the gospel! Of that little group, all went on in their faith. I went into the ministry and another, Francis Chaplin, spent thirty years as a missionary in Bolivia with the Bolivian Indian Mission.'

'Almost seventy years after the events of that remarkable revival in Lowestoft, I can identify at least three marks of the revival: a coming together of spiritually-minded people, irrespective of their church labels; a renunciation of all that was offensive to God's law, and a sincere following of the Scriptures.'

Henry Hannant recalls that those who met in the schoolroom for prayer every Monday evening for the six months prior to the revival concerned themselves with nothing but prayer for revival. At these meetings there was a real atmosphere and a sense of the presence of the Lord. The effect of the Wednesday evening meeting was quite unexpected and when the sixty or seventy people walked down the two aisles in response to the invitation it was 'to the amazement of everyone.' He describes some of the meetings in the Baptist Church when people sat on the windowsills and pulpit steps; and the same happened in St John's, where eight hundred people pushed into the large building.

The revival lasted only a month, but the results continued for years afterwards both in East Anglia and in Scotland. There are definite records of over five hundred conversions, and the Baptist Church membership increased by thirty-eight in 1921, though, of course, others followed in later years as a result of their conversion during the revival. For a long time afterwards the church was alive and the prayer meetings doubled in attendance.

Chapter 9

I was there: Lewis (Scotland) 1949

This is an account of the revival in the Isle of Lewis between 1949 and 1952. Lewis is one of the Hebridean islands off the west coast of Scotland and it had experienced many revivals during the nineteenth century and earlier in the twentieth century. The record here is taken from the witness of those who were personally involved; their stories are recorded on a cassette issued by Ambassador Productions Ltd of Belfast, under the title Lewis—Land of Revival. In 1949 Duncan Campbell visited the island to conduct a two-week evangelistic mission and stayed for two years.

In 1949 a new minister came to the parish of Barvas and decided to spend two nights a week in prayer. For three months he spent Tuesdays and Fridays in a barn with a few praying members. One evening they broke through in prayer and 'A power was let loose that shook the Hebrides.' Soon there was a hunger and a life in the congregation and 'a fantastic liveliness in the prayer meetings'. For the first two weeks of Duncan's mission no one was converted and then, on the last night, seven young people made a commitment to Christ. At the end of this service the benediction was pronounced and it was suggested that the congregation should go home; but when they went to the door of the church, a great crowd of people was gathering as if drawn by an unseen hand. Soon the church was packed, even the pulpit stairs were crowded, and people were crying to God for mercy. The minister gave out the metrical Psalm 102: 'When Zion's bondage God turned back...', and one Christian present comments: 'We sang and we sang and we sang ... You were aware of the Spirit of the Lord just there.' The minister eventually sent everyone home but announced that there would be another meeting in about an hour in the home of Mr McDougall. Crowds packed into this home and many were converted.

Duncan Campbell's method was to preach on sin, condemnation and hell during the services, but to reserve the way of salvation for the after-meetings attended only by those who were genuinely seeking the way of salvation. He did not preach the gospel to those who were uninterested until they were under conviction; then he showed them the loveliness of Christ and salvation.

Whole families were transformed and sometimes would spend a full Saturday in prayer and praise. One man, who was only eleven years old at the time of the revival, recalls that his knowledge of Christianity was limited to what he had learnt at school; he had never been to Sunday School and only once to church. One morning he woke up to a quiet house as if someone was ill; he was told to be quiet because his father had been converted and wanted to read the Bible. He remembers his mother searching the shelves for the long-neglected Bible and unwrapping it from its old cloth. This was the first time the young boy had seen the Bible in his home. The whole home was changed and even the visitors to the house changed and Duncan Campbell himself stayed there. Listening to Campbell preaching, this young boy was aware of God searching him deeply: 'I managed to push it away, though many were saved around me. I was converted the following year.'

This revival cannot be explained in terms of mere emotionalism. A deep and lasting work was done in the lives of many, and in the same meeting that some were saved, others could go away challenged but resisting. Some never came to Christ although it was generally agreed they 'could never be the same again'.

The Spirit of God was moving through the island, often far away from the churches. Early in the revival one minister felt compelled to leave a meeting and go to a local dance hall where many of the young people had gathered. He arrived just as there was a lull in the dancing and everyone was sitting down. When the minister, Mr McClelland, entered, the young man who was master of ceremonies was angry and ordered him out, demanding, 'Have you got a ticket to come in?' 'No', replied the minister, 'but I have a ticket to take me anywhere.' The MC was so angry he had to be restrained by his mother from hitting the minister! Instead he called for a dance, but no one moved. Mr McClelland invited the young girl who had just been singing to join him in a psalm, and they began to sing Psalm 139: 'Whither from thy Spirit shall I flee...?' Young people were in tears, and before the psalm was finished the MC was converted. He went to the minister, apologized and then rushed outside: 'It was just as if something hit me. I now know what it was, it was the power of God in that place. I went into the bus outside and wept my eyes out.'

The whole island was aware of God. 'It seemed as if the very air was electrified with the Spirit of God ... There was an awesomeness of the presence of God,' so much so that many were terrified of being converted. Some refused to come to the meetings, but God met them in the fields; others sat near the door so that they could make a fast escape, but still they were converted. 'Revival can be a terrible thing,' comments one, 'to be face to face with God.' A young girl found herself in a home where all the talk was about those who had been converted: 'I got up and walked out because I was afraid I might get converted.'

One of the most wonderful things for many was the desire of the young people to attend church and read the Bible. Places of pleasure were closed because there were so few who wanted to attend. 'A whole generation was touched, many rejected and turned away, but they could never be the same again.' The revival affected every part of life and gave a new hunger for spiritual things. One man went home after a meeting but could not sleep: 'At 2.00 a.m. I asked God to take me as I am. Next morning everything was different; there seemed to be a change even in the ragged beauty of the village. All day I was longing for the meeting that evening.' Another comments: 'It didn't matter what you were doing, you were just longing for the prayer meeting.'

Those who witnessed the revival never had any doubt about its genuineness and the lasting value of its fruit. One claimed, 'The characteristic of revival that is not true of a campaign is that very few go back into the world.' In one church alone, three years later, most of the members were the fruit of the revival. Yet many found it impossible to describe what it was like to be in revival; it went beyond words. The power of the preaching and singing, the awesome presence of God, the packed congregations and prayer meetings, people crying for mercy or praising God for a new-found salvation—and all this to a degree unknown normally. One eye-witness comments: 'You cannot explain revival to those who have never experienced it. In revival God is completely in control, and the whole community is aware of that.' Another concluded: 'You were brought into touch with the powers of the world to come, and you will never be content with anything less.'

Duncan Campbell himself describes a prayer meeting in one village. There had been bitter opposition in the village, and although many attended the meetings from other areas, very few locals attended because of the opposition of the minister. A church leader suggested they should go to prayer, and thirty or so moved into the home of a friendly farmer. Prayer was hard, and about midnight Duncan Campbell turned to the local blacksmith, who had been silent so far, and said, 'I feel the time has come when you ought to pray.' The man prayed for about half an hour, 'because in revival time doesn't matter', and then drew his prayer to a close with a bold challenge: 'God, do you not know that your honour is at stake? You promised to pour floods on dry ground, and you are not doing it.' He paused for a while and then concluded: 'God, your honour is at stake, and I challenge you to keep your covenant engagements.' At that moment, Duncan Campbell recalls, 'That whole granite house shook like a leaf,' and whilst one elder thought of an earth tremor, Duncan was reminded of Acts 4:31: 'After they prayed, the place where they were meeting was shaken…'

Duncan Campbell pronounced the benediction and they went outside. It was about two o'clock in the morning and they found 'the whole village alive, ablaze with God'. Men and women were carrying chairs and asking if there was room in the church for them!

A few years later Duncan returned to that village and an elder pointed out to him a house, boarded up. 'That', the elder commented, 'was the drinking house and it has never been opened since the revival; last night fourteen men who frequented that building were praying in the church prayer meeting.' Duncan Campbell commented simply: 'Very remarkable things happen when God moves in revival.'

I was there—revival in the Hebrides (Lewis), Scotland

The following is a summary of a transcript of a sermon preached by Duncan Campbell of the Faith Mission in Edinburgh on 10 October 1958 on the subject of 'revival in the Hebrides'. It is his own personal record as the one whom God used significantly in this revival.

The islands of Lewis and Harris had been through a time of steep spiritual decline among all ages. The minister of the parish church of Barra, together with a few men and two women (Peggy and Christine aged 84 and 82) entered into a solemn covenant with God to pray. They prayed for months, and nothing happened. One night, while the men were praying in a barn, a young man read from Psalm 24:

'Who shall ascend the hill of God, and who shall stand in his holy presence? He that hath clean hands and a pure heart, who hath not lifted up his soul unto vanity or sworn deceitfully; he shall receive the blessing of the LORD.'

The young man turned to his companions: 'Brethren, it seems to me just so much humbug waiting as we are waiting, praying, as we are praying, unless we ourselves are rightly related to God.' He then began to pray earnestly, and in a moment 'A power was let loose that shook the parish centre to circumference'. At that very hour, the two sisters were praying in their cottage four miles away, and one had a vision from God of churches crowded and the young people flocking to the place of worship. They urged the minister to send for Duncan Campbell.

Duncan Campbell arrived on the island in 1949. This first meeting began at 9 pm and was 'very ordinary'. One of the Elders suggested, 'Mr Campbell, I hope you are not disappointed that revival has not broken. God has promised; he is a covenant keeping God; he must be true to his covenant engagements and revival is going to come and is going to sweep this parish.' The Elder then prayed and kept repeating 'Lord, you dare not fail us. You must not fail us. You have promised; you must fulfil your promise. Hast thou not said, "I will pour water on the thirsty, and floods upon the dry ground."? Your honour is at stake.' The people sang the opening verse of Psalm 102 and when Duncan Campbell went to the door of the church, there were six or seven hundred people waiting to come in! The meeting continued until 4 o'clock in the morning and scores were crying, 'God be merciful to me, the sinner'. One farmer cried out 'O God, I feel that hell itself is too good for me.'

At that early hour, people were also gathering at the police station and as Duncan Campbell made his way there men and women were on the roadside kneeling and weeping. 'God swept through that gathering, and many were brought to a saving knowledge of the truth before they left that hallowed spot.' For five weeks, the Spirit of God continued his work with packed churches until the early hours. Then the movement swept into neighbouring parishes. People came from a distance of over sixty miles to the meetings.

What were the main features of the revival? 'First I would mention a sense of God that lays hold of the community ... In revival God sweeps into the community and the whole community is caught up in an overwhelming sense of God. God becomes real, when the fear of God lays hold upon men, when things eternal loom large in their vision and the general topic of conversation among young and old, is the way of salvation.'

A businessman who never attended church, and had very little thought for God, arrived from the mainland. His testimony was that as soon as he stepped onto the island: 'I was suddenly made conscious of God, and before I arrived at the main road, God met with me and saved me. At that moment I entered into a saving relationship with Jesus Christ.' A young man, out in the field, feeding sheep, suddenly began to tremble and cry. He became conscious of his sin, and beside a stone in the open field, he cried out: 'Lord, if it's my surrender you want, you have it now.' A group of young men out on the hills discussing the amount of beer they will need at the end of the week, were suddenly conscious of God and, with no preacher, no meeting, no word about revival, God came into them, and within minutes they were brought to a saving knowledge of Jesus Christ. Campbell adds, 'It was my privilege and pleasure recently to be at a meeting when they all took part in prayer ... Eight of them are today office-bearers in the local church there, three of them Elders and four of them Deacons.'

The parish minister of Barra recorded, 'walking along the road or conversing with people on the hillside, one was conscious of a Presence that could not be explained from any human angle, so real, so wonderful was this sense of God.'

The second main feature was a deep conviction of sin: 'I can remember being in a meeting one evening when the cry of the penitent was so terrible, so awful, that it was necessary for me to stop preaching and endeavour in some way to help. I saw as many as twenty-seven men lying prostrate on the ground, crying in great distress that God might have mercy on them.'

On one occasion the two elderly sisters urged Duncan Campbell to go to a particular district on the island that was resistant to revival. He felt no inclination to go and said so. He received the reply: 'Mr Campbell, if you were living nearer to the Saviour, perhaps he will reveal his secrets to you also.' They prayed together and Peggy began her prayer like this: 'Lord, you remember the conversation that I had with you this morning and how you revealed to me that seven men in this village were going to become pillars in the House of God. I have delivered your message to the Minister here, but he is not prepared to accept it. You give him wisdom because he badly needs it. You promised and you must fulfil your promise. If you do not give me the seven men that you promised, how am I going to trust you again?' Duncan Campbell assured her he would go, to which she responded 'you had better.'

In that village a large congregation was waiting for him in a home. He had been preaching only fifteen minutes from Acts 17:30–31 when so many were in distress that he had to stop. Among those crying to God for mercy were Peggy's seven men 'prostrate on their faces before God'. Two of the young men were pipers due to play at a dance that evening. The minister went to the dance hall and told the young people of the conversion of their pipers and 'the power of God swept into the dance hall and in a matter minutes the music gave place to the cry of young men and women seeking the way of salvation. The hall emptied and the young people made their way home. Sometime later Duncan learned that only three or four of those young people remained unsaved.

On the island of Benbecula, 'Things were very hard and difficult, the people were not disposed to attend the meetings at all, and one felt that we were up against a stone wall.' People prayed, and particularly one young man prayed so earnestly and God swept through the island. 'Men who were out fishing left their fishing boats and made for the church. Others who were labouring at the peat banks left the peat banks and made for the church. A schoolmaster setting examination papers in his home, left his papers, took his car, motored fifteen miles, crossed a ferry and arrived during the midnight meeting and within a matter of ten minutes was gloriously saved ... Men and women were found in distress by the roadside, in the churches, in homes, on the hillsides—indeed the whole island was in the grip of God.' Three years after this, the young people were found in the prayer meetings rather than the picture and dance halls. When revisiting the island some years later, the minister offered to show Duncan 'Flowers of wonderful fragrance'. He led him to the drawing room of his home: 'Where I found between twenty-five and thirty young men and women on their knees in prayer, praying for their island, praying for the parish, praying for their church, but especially pray that the anointing of God would fall upon the Minister.' Elsewhere in the district of Arran, as a result of the revival, the public house was closed and the young men who frequented it were in the prayer meeting. In another congregation, the minister could point to twenty young men in the prayer meeting and another fifteen in the row behind them—all converts of the revival.

Asked, 'Do the converts stand?' Duncan Campbell commented, 'It is not a question of ministers organising meetings and endeavouring to get young people to attend them; it is a matter of the young people organising meetings and asking the ministers to attend them!'

I was there: The Congo (Zaire) 1953

David Davies was a missionary with the World Evangelization Crusade in the Belgian Congo from 1937. He was still in the Congo when revival came in 1953 and later he and his wife were under house arrest during the Simba rebellion in 1964.

'When God comes in revival power it is different from anything you can imagine. This is not a campaign, nor a mission; and it is not something whipped up either. Revival is when God comes down in his presence.'

'I was the leading missionary in my station, and we had one hundred and thirty churches in our area. They were busy churches with plenty of activity. We had many meetings, a medical work, and hundreds of children in the mission schools. But people were cooling off; they did not come to the prayer meeting and Bible study as they used to. Without a doubt salvation was there and people were converted, but something was missing. We were rather like Lazarus, out of the grave but with hands and feet wrapped around with a towel. One missionary put it simply: "We have a good shop window."'

'Someone urged the missionaries to spend one whole day each month in prayer, and many took this up. As a result, a number of us became aware that we were not burning for God. Missionaries realized there were wrong relationships and they got right with each other, and then we got right with the national evangelists and pastors who asked to join us in prayer. But this was not revival.'

'The revival actually began in the mission station at Lubutu, more than five hundred miles from where I worked. It was the Saturday night Bible study and prayer meeting. For some time the study had been in the Acts of the Apostles and centred on the working of God in the early church. The missionaries were concerned that there was no freedom in prayer and the meeting was hard going. Then one pastor broke down and wept. This was a very unusual thing. He explained that he had a hardness of heart, and as he shared, so the conviction spread until there was sobbing, wailing, groaning and even shrieking, from all over the meeting. This was extreme to the missionaries present! Africans were on their faces crying and praying; the whole place seemed to be bedlam. I am reminded now that Charles Haddon Spurgeon once prayed, "Lord, send us a season of glorious disorder." The missionaries tried to quieten everything down, but they failed and the meeting went on until two o'clock in the morning.'

'Letters began to arrive on other mission stations describing the happenings at Lubutu. Now it was my turn to doubt. I was receiving letters from my brother that troubled me because of the extreme language that he used to describe what was happening. The revival had begun in Lubutu in January 1953; by May it had spread to my brother's station, one hundred and sixty miles away, and by July it reached me at Wamba, a further two hundred and sixty miles. And so it went on and on. The revival spread like a bush fire for hundreds of miles, and other missions were touched by it.'

'My church had sent an evangelist down to Lubutu at the end of his training, and he was there when the revival came. On his first Sunday back with us he preached on Exodus 19:10–11: "And the Lord said to Moses, 'Go to the people and consecrate them today and tomorrow. Have them wash their clothes and be ready by the third day, because on that day the Lord will come down on Mount Sinai in the sight of all the people.'" It was a powerful message, but nothing happened so I gave out the last hymn and the benediction and then invited any who needed counsel to stay in their seat. As the congregation was leaving, a young teacher came and sat right at the front; he shook uncontrollably and was sobbing. A young cripple girl suddenly began screaming, "What shall I do? What shall I do? I'm going to hell!" People came running back into the church. The girl was known as a good Christian, but she was convicted of cheating a shopkeeper. The young man was guilty of jealousy, a little thing to many, but it terrified him.'

'I was counselling those who were crying for help when an African ran in with the urgent message that my wife needed me at the house. I found the place full of people; the head man, a good Christian, was lying on the floor twisting and turning in agony, and crying over and over, "What shall I do? What shall I do?" After a while he confessed everything and declared with joy, "My heart is clean. I claim forgiveness through the death and blood of Jesus Christ my Lord." In a moment everyone present was claiming forgiveness with a radiant joy, and we all returned to the church for another meeting! The next day was a day for putting things right with one another. Suddenly God had come down and it was a visitation from heaven.'

'At this time, God moved in powerful ways. I wrote a letter to an evangelist two hundred miles away; all I intended to do was to tell him what was happening here at Wamba, but as soon as he read the letter he came under the power of God. He shared the letter with his church and the Spirit came upon them also. We were not in control; God was, and everything was in perfect order.

'At this time it was a revival amongst God's people; very few unbelievers were saved for the first two or three months. God was cleansing the church first. Hearts were being searched. Some people had sins that had been hidden for years, and they had come to the conclusion that these sins did not matter. God was dealing with individuals painfully. By this time the whole town was talking about God.'

'Sometimes conviction could be a terrible thing and those who resisted suffered most. An evangelist went into a coma for three days. Another woman went mad under conviction until she confessed her sin. This was the price for some of hiding sin and resisting God. We wondered at some of the strange things that happened during the revival, and only felt safe if we could find a scriptural parallel. Some Christians saw a strange light over the preachers, and we found such a light in the conversion of Saul of Tarsus. The terrible shaking and trembling experienced by some had parallels in the lives of Moses and David, and John who "fell as one dead" before the Saviour. Others seemed to be transfixed and could not open their hands; this too had a counterpart in the life of Jeroboam recorded in 1 Kings 13. The phenomena soon passed, but the lasting fruits of the revival were such things as holiness, tenderness, a love for the Bible and prayer and an exaltation of the person and work of Christ.'

'The Christians all came to the meetings, which could go on for a long time. It was not unusual for a Bible Study to begin at 6.30 in the morning and still to be in progress at noon. People talked in whispers because they felt God near. One missionary wrote home, "We seem to be wrapped around by the presence of God." I have been in meetings where God was so real that you hardly dared to sit on a chair. I was reminded of Job 42:5: "My ears had heard of you, but now my eyes have seen you." The Word of God was powerful now, but this was not an altogether new thing amongst us. We had saturated our people in the Word of God for a long time and when the revival came the value of this was clearly seen. People who had left the schools years before could be working in a garden miles away from any Christian church, yet God came to them and brought verses to their memory.'

'The reformation that resulted from this revival was wonderful. Many had stolen from the state, and the Christians and converts wanted to make restitution. So many things were being returned to the Belgian Office that an embarrassed official wrote to me: "Mr Davies, I've no time to handle all this. Tell them to come to your mission and fill a truck and you bring a load down." God is light and people could not live in fellowship with him if they were unholy.'

'Hymns were written during the revival, some of them given directly by God. And people prayed as never before. Simultaneous praying was a common thing in the revival, but it never seemed to be out of place or disorderly. The people also had a passion for evangelism. One Sunday it was announced in church that the following week the meeting would be held outside. And this went on every alternate Sunday for a long time. Even pagans wanted the Christians to go to their village to hold a service. People were saved by the hundreds and thousands as the church moved out.'

'And did it last? I kept a diary for eighteen months, and at the end of that time the power of God was still there. Thirty years later the leaders of the churches are those who were blessed by the revival. But there is a new generation that needs its own revival because, "Another generation grew up, who knew neither the Lord nor what he had done for Israel" (Judges 2:10). But you cannot pray for revival to come to your church unless you are willing for it to come to you personally.'

I was there: East Java (Indonesia) 1972

The following report is taken from an interview at the home of Colin and Joan Waltham in Leigh-on-Sea, Essex, on 25 August 1989. It concerns their experience during the early 1970s whilst they were serving as missionaries at Madiun, the administrative capital of eastern Java in Indonesia.

Madiun, the administrative capital of East Java, boasts a large sugar factory and little else. Colin and Joan arrived in time for Christmas 1970. Like most of Indonesia, the population of Madiun is largely Muslim with a few Hindus, though traditional animism clings tightly to both. The Christian fellowship in the church where they served consisted of around sixty members, none of whom was more than seven years old in the faith and all of whom knew the meaning of suffering for the gospel. Many widows had struggled to bring up a family after their husbands had 'disappeared' in the aftermath of the attempted Communist coup in 1965. Since then, Muslim opposition to the Christians had only stiffened their resolve to be faithful to Christ. The church was firmly evangelical, simply taking God at his word, and keenly evangelistic, bringing the gospel regularly into surrounding villages.

Villages that could boast a market square were the focal point of life and commerce for the villages scattered around them. Village work formed the chief part of Colin's ministry, and although only five or six 'market villages' had a small group of Christians gathering regularly, the gospel was preached in thirty more. A table would be set up with tracts, Bibles and Christian books and, forbidden by law to preach directly, Colin, together with another missionary and the young evangelists from Madiun, they would simply explain the books they had for sale. Opposition came from the people, the police, the Muslim leader, or the local chief, but often a crowd of fifty or one hundred would give a noisy and sometimes abusive attention. Those interested would ask to be taught more; a few came to Christ, but not many.

Gradually Colin and Joan were identified with the people and accepted by them. Their acceptance was increased even further when everything movable was stolen from their home whilst Colin was preaching on the text: 'Do not worry saying, "What shall we eat?" or, "What shall we drink?" or, "What shall we wear?" For the pagans ran after all these things'!

The poverty of the area can be measured by the fact that in one village Colin was approached by the head man who remarked how wealthy the missionary was to own his own toothbrush; in that place a communal brush hung on a piece of string in the centre of the village! The household rubbish, tipped out from the home of Colin and Joan, was searched through by their young girl helper; when she had had her pickings the rickshaw drivers moved in and they were in turn followed by the beggars, until there was nothing left. In a very dry season when the crops failed people frequently starved.

By 1972 the church had outgrown their hired building and the people purchased a large roofless factory to rebuild. The sacrificial giving of these desperately poor people was remarkable. The Christians gave everything they had for their new building which would seat three hundred people. If they had a spare shirt, or an extra chair, they sold it to buy bricks. When the bricks had been purchased, the members built with their own labour. They used to meet at five o'clock each morning to pray for more bricks, and when they had sufficient bricks they continued to pray for people to fill their new building. The people hurt themselves to build their meeting-place.

The Christians were not specifically praying for revival, but they so sincerely loved Christ that they lived in the light of his presence among them. With a simple faith that God always keeps his promise, they practised the presence of Christ and were 'at ease in Jesus'. During the summer of 1972 about thirty of the young people were gathered for a week of intensive Bible teaching. During a time of testimony and prayer they were suddenly broken, and with crying and confession many grievances

162 Praying for Revival

and grudges were put right. It was the beginning of a new work of God among the people.

The church building was ready by September and shortly after its opening the Spirit began to move among the whole congregation as he had among the young people. Evil attitudes and thoughts were confessed, cherished charms were thrown away, and Warcito, a blind lad, had his sight restored. Healing was not a significant part of this work, but God moved in the lives of a few to restore them physically. Barriers seemed to fall away, and the church, normally a caring and loving people though sensitive and easily offended, now experienced a depth of love and a reality of faith unknown before. Rivalry disappeared and all evangelized as one.

Over the next six months there was much evidence of the work of the Spirit spilling over into the community. A young girl stood up to give her testimony in a market village, an outrageous thing in a Muslim community, and yet some of the villagers professed faith in Christ. In the mountain village of Ngravyen someone left a copy of the tract *Four things God wants you to know*. Because it was the wet season Colin was unable to return until three months later, when he found forty believers waiting for him. An old man went to the village of Baturettno in the valley and led fifty to Christ. Startled by this, the church in Madiun sent Radjum, a mature evangelist, to verify the work in Baturettno. Even village chiefs began to ask for evangelists to come and preach to them. All down the valley people were aware of the work of God, and at least one witchdoctor was so impressed by the power of Christ that he began to use the sign of the cross in his efforts to heal and help people. Many were converted and when the churches in the valley required two thousand members to register with the Indonesian government, they had no difficulty in mustering that number.

For two to three months there was incredible effectiveness in evangelism, but towards the middle of 1973 the work settled into a gradual and less spectacular growth. However, the lives of the Christians had become 'beautiful for Jesus' and they loved to worship and learn from Scripture; one blind lady regularly walked three miles to church, even though her Islamic neighbours often literally threw obstacles in her path to trip her up.

Colin and Joan found themselves in the middle of a work that was beyond their own power to control. 'It was like watching television,' they claim; God was working, and they felt they had little to do with it. Sometimes Colin would go to a village to preach and nothing would happen, but when he came home he learned that the Spirit had been working in another village. God was not using the missionary to lead people to Christ, but the whole church was motivated to talk about the gospel. Colin found himself called upon to teach young believers everywhere. Rising at four in the morning and reaching home at midnight, he was trying to visit thirty-six villages in a month. Yet in spite of this programme, both Colin and Joan claim that in the revival, which they were too busy at the time to recognize as revival, 'We learnt to be lazy Christians; we learnt to wait and see what Jesus does before we do anything ourselves.' By the end of the revival there were groups of believers meeting in more than thirty villages.

There is something that can never be lost, even with the passing of time, from those who experience revival. Colin and Joan were given an awareness of what God can do, and a love for Christ, and from Christ, that they can never forget. God taught them lessons from the Indonesian Christians, who knew nothing of Western sophistication, but simply trusted that what God said he meant. There were no human methods, and numbers were not relevant. Colin is convinced that 'Since revival is totally in the sovereign plan of God, numbers don't count.' But for those who have lived through revival life can in some ways be very lonely afterwards. Very few, whether missionaries or ministers, can really understand what revival is, or how different Christian life and service are in revival times. In an age when our activity and methods count for so much, few can understand what it is like when God saturates his people.

I was there: Oradea, Romania

THE SECOND BAPTIST CHURCH 1972–1977

This personal account of revival in Romania comes from Zorica, the wife of George Ghiță Gheorghiaș, and was translated by Oana Crenicean-Tudoran MACI. Zorica was a young schoolgirl at the time of the revival.

During the 1970s brother Covaci, the pastor of the Second Baptist Church in Oradea, was nearing retirement. This made him want to be on good terms with the Communist Securitate whose informants were infiltrated everywhere, even in the Second Baptist Church. At the same time, pastor Covaci did not want to antagonise the church fellowship. In his love towards God, he was trying to please both parties. Sadly, the church was worldly and the brothers more worldly than spiritual. Alcohol use was common among them. Many of the men stopped by a public house called Calul Bălan (The Fair Horse) for a drink on their way to church.

The church youth found out about this and took the pastor to task about the worldly attitude of the so-called 'Christians'. Pastor Covaci was aware of all this, but could not find the strength to deal with it, so he agreed for the church to pray for another pastor to step in and set things right. The Elders, led by brother Coltea, and the church youth, called the church to pray for a brother, Liviu Olah who was a young lawyer from Timișoara and who had been involved in mission work around Timișoara with the youth in that city. They prayed for nearly six months.

Liviu Olah came to preach at the Second Baptist Church in 1972. His sermon was full of the power of the Holy Spirit, and his humble attitude touched everyone. You could feel and see the anointing of the Holy Spirit over this man. He attended the youth prayer groups as well as house groups and church prayer meetings; he urged everyone to pray without ceasing. Believers started to gather as early as 5:30am for prayer and intercession before going to work. This was during Communism, yet people did not feel afraid or ashamed to meet at dawn every day. Liviu taught us to have prayer lists and prayer and fasting chains for every issue and person we brought before God. The Lord answered prayers and there was much joy. Prayer was at the heart of the revival. All the problems of the church, as well as of every individual, were brought before the Lord, day and night.

The sermons of brother Liviu were short, fifteen or twenty minutes, but very powerful. No one could resist his appeals, especially when, at the end of a sermon, he would call on the audience to surrender themselves to God with all their problems. When the sermon was over, the men's choir started singing familiar hymns, and this became customary for this type of event. Then brother Olah spoke with such power that you could hear people crying and weeping as they were being convicted by the word of God.

Hundreds of people repented. Every few weeks dozens of converts were baptised. On one special day one hundred and twenty were baptised. The church grew rapidly, so the old building became too small. It was impossible to get a seat unless you turned up an hour before the start of the service and it was hard to press through the crowd of people who had been standing for hours. Whenever anyone needed to leave, a sort of a 'wave' was set in motion and it was almost impossible to walk out. The oxygen would run out due to the sheer size of the crowd, so that even during winter doors and windows had to be kept wide open.

People from all around Oradea and the nearby villages came to faith, even from as far as Sibiu, Braşov, Suceava, Bucureşti, Constanţa, Caransebeş. The revival enveloped the entire country (perhaps not as intensely as in Oradea), but many came out of curiosity to see and hear what was happening at the Second Baptist Church in Oradea. Many Baptist and Pentecostal churches were transformed by this revival. All who attended the services returned home with enthusiasm and full of the desire to continue living the kind of spiritual experience they had just had. Soon after, evangelism and children's ministries began. Paul and Delia Negrut, Viorel Oros, Maria Bodor, Maria Cornea, Angela Maior and others were in charge of children's ministries. This then spread, and many churches from around the country started their own local ministries.

Lives and habits were changed. I remember pastor Liviu preaching about the brothers calling into the public house on their way to church; he was crying over this sin and pleaded in tears: 'Brothers, we cannot be slapping Christ in the face by doing this!' He cried as if it was his own sin. When Liviu Olah preached and sang, his shirt and jacket were drenched in sweat. He needed another change of clothes after the services. He identified with the sin of the people, just as Daniel did when he prayed for his people. The brothers were so moved and convicted by the words and manner of brother Liviu Olah, that they stopped going to the public house. A short while after, that place closed.

Around the same time that the revival began, government repression also started. Brother Liviu Olah and others were harassed by the Securitate, who put huge pressure on him to leave the country. This was unsuccessful at first, although around 1977 brother Olah was eventually forced to escape to the United States.

The blessed outcome of the revival was the healthy spiritual growth of the Baptist and Pentecostal believers. Many youth groups went on missions every Sunday, not just around the villages in the county, but beyond, in other counties. There was a desire to serve other communities where there weren't as many believers. Everyone burned with the desire of taking the Good News of salvation to all around them. Christians—even schoolchildren who became Christians—witnessed to their colleagues at work or school without fear, though many were pursued and harassed by the Securitate. I went through such an experience after I became a believer. The new followers gathered during the week in house groups and lifted up fervent prayers to the Lord.

In 1978, brother Iosif Ţon came from Ploieşti. The Lord brought him to Oradea; he was gifted in teaching. The crowd of new converts now needed healthy and solid teaching from the word of God. I was at school in Oradea and did everything I could to attend church gatherings. I loved going to the Bible studies for the youth on Monday evenings by brother Ţon. Many of us grew in faith through these and became involved in ministry with the churches we belonged to. We used to go home on Saturdays (when we didn't have sporting events) and bring the children together to teach them lessons from the Bible. The generation touched by this wonderful revival was also the one to have started youth ministries in the churches around Romania.

For me, revival is a powerful 'overhaul' of the 'Christians' in a certain area, prompted by the Holy Spirit. It must always start with the repentance of the believers. Only then can others be touched. An authentic revival significantly affects the social and economic life of the area also. In revival, the believers lose any sense of shame or fear of witnessing. I remember one day I was walking to school and an elderly sister from church walked up to me and said: 'My dear, I'd like to invite you to come to the Second Church on Simion Bărnuţiu Road for an evangelistic event.' The sister did not know I attended there regularly. I was so impressed by the boldness of this lady to invite to church people whom she had only come across. Another effect of this revival was that people asked God for great things though prayer. They prayed for the word to be preached in stadiums and on the radio, which was like science-fiction at the time. But, this happened when Billy Graham came to Romania in 1985 and Luis Palau five years later.

I was there: Bury St Edmunds 1980–1985

WESTGATE CHAPEL

Bob Cotton was the pastor at Westgate Evangelical Church from its foundation until he was appointed Director for the European Missionary Fellowship in 1985. The church began as a plant from a village church, Barrow Congregational Chapel, some eight miles east towards Newmarket where Bob was pastor. As his congregation grew, he realised that ten homes were represented from Bury St Edmunds; this was sufficient to commence a church in that town. Twenty-five members, with an average age of thirty, began the work with prayer meetings in a home and in February 1975 regular Sunday services commenced. This is Bob's report:

'From 1975–1980, a solid gospel work developed in Bury and the membership increased; however, to our dismay and discouragement, there were few real conversions during this period. With a longing for more and a breakthrough to confirm our move from village to town, I attended the Bala Ministers Conference in North Wales in 1979. The main speaker was Derek Swann from Ashford Congregational Church in Middlesex and he spent some time outlining the 'Concert for Prayer'. In October 1774 ministers in Scotland had been deeply concerned for the lack of spiritual life in their congregations and they covenanted to pray 'in concert' on Saturday evening and Sunday morning and for extended times of prayer on the first Tuesday in April, August and November. Jonathan Edwards in America heard of this and preached a sermon that was published under the title *An Humble Attempt...*[66] This 'Concert of Prayer' led to the 'Great Awakening' on both sides of the Atlantic in the eighteenth century.

Arriving home, I felt compelled to call together the church at Bury for more concentrated prayer and self-examination, pleading with God to

---

66 See pp. 186 ff for more on the 'concert of prayer' and Jonathan Edwards' *Humble Attempt...*

deal with us to make us fit to bear His gospel. I had a burning desire for God to come among us and this soon spread throughout the fellowship. Special meetings were arranged to consider our situation and our personal walk with God. We earnestly sought the Lord regarding our future evangelism in the town and the salvation of some twenty unconverted young people in our fellowship. They were extraordinary meetings of self-examination. They started as a prayer meeting but became more of an 'experience meeting' as we expressed and confessed our own failures, sinfulness, lethargy and spiritual coldness. There were tears and then challenge as the Lord Himself broke into our fellowship causing the pastor and people alike to look more closely into our hearts and attitudes. We commenced Saturday morning prayer meetings, particularly designed to beseech God for souls to be saved. Roughly half our congregation of forty would be present.

We soon became aware that something different was happening among us. There was a stirring and a few professions of faith. At that time I thought this was the norm for any gospel-based church. Among the first to be converted was a couple from a Hindu and nominal Christian background. After attending Westgate Chapel Dr Kiru recalls breaking down in tears at home and crying out: 'Lord, I am ashamed that I have ignored you all these years. Please forgive me of my sins and let me be a witness for Thee.' He added 'I felt a warmth in my heart and knew that I was saved and my sins had been forgiven … I experienced a joy that I had not experienced before.' Sheila, a housewife and mother, was invited to the mission 'Faith for our Times' in September 1980 and realised that it was not 'something' that was missing from her life, but 'someone'. Within a week Sheila had trusted Christ and felt 'a quiet assurance within that the Lord had forgiven me and that I was a child of his.'

An exceptional time began in the Spring of 1980 and culminated in a season of refreshing from the presence of the Lord. We had a great expectation of conversions beyond the experience of any of us. There was an obvious perceptible presence of God among us at every service, especially during and after the preaching of the gospel. One Sunday in September 1980 there was an unusual outpouring of God's Spirit, with several people converted between the two services. After the evening service I went into the church hall to find several in tears and calling out: 'Lord, help me!' Twenty came into personal faith that evening. My son wrote in his diary: 'Today, God came to Bury St Edmunds.' Within five months over fifty found a saving knowledge of Jesus.

The blessing of God was richly known and felt and continued at a lesser level of intensity for five years. Remarkable experiences were the norm rather than the exception as we witnessed regular conversions to Christ and the restoration of backsliding believers. We were aware of a thorough transforming work rather than emotional, temporary and superficial commitments. There were conversions among all ages and classes, from teenagers to a lady of eighty-two years who had not been to church for half a century; housewives, labourers and professionals came to a saving faith. The great majority of those who were restored or saved at that time, have continued well with the Lord.

Some opposition and criticism began to be expressed from folk within our fellowship who were from a hard-line Reformed background. They felt that Westgate was encouraging emotionalism, and a few of these left us. Elsewhere, there were murmurs and rumours that came back to me from members of other local churches that 'Westgate was now charismatic'!

I have been reluctant to describe this as a revival because it was not a community saturated with the awesome presence of God with many signs and extraordinary phenomena attending. We were seeing localised showers, mainly of people who came to the services straight out of the world, were converted and added to the church. We preferred to refer to that time as 'a season of refreshing'. A harvest after much sowing, weeping and praying. There was one common feature about all those conversions: it was the utter brokenness, accompanied by tears and repentance, and then great joy. What happened during this period brought about a change in the church generally—the preaching, evangelism, personal witnessing and of course, praying. There was such expectation week by week as we came together; so much so that many did not want to be away for holidays or sickness. The question was always asked on return: 'What have we missed?'

What began as an evangelistic mission established a vibrant living New Testament church. After five years of plenty we moved to virtually nothing in the way of conversions. It appeared to me that this ended as suddenly as it had arrived, although outwardly we were carrying on as usual. It seemed that 'God turned off the tap'. I do not know why, and I have often thought about it. But it left a strong witness in the town, where preaching the pure gospel of the grace of God was paramount. We kept no records of numbers that I am aware of at this time, although I believe the congregation doubled and membership rose from twenty-five to around eighty.'

I was there: Ambt Delden, Netherlands, June 2006

Hans Pieterman, a Dutch Christian now living with his wife Aletta in Germany, has had a long and deep concern for true revival. He gathered personal reflections of a divine visitation in June 2006 at a revival convention in Ambt Delden, the Netherlands (Holland).

During the 1990s meetings for young people on Saturday evening were held in Holland, led by ministers of the Reformed churches and with much blessing of the Lord. About the year 2000 a group of young people from the Reformed churches in the Alblasserwaard started to pray for revival every Saturday morning, eventually some forty attending. They also began youth meetings in Hardinxveld and subsequently in other towns also. These meetings consisted mainly of preaching, lecturing and asking questions. Not infrequently the meetings were attended by a real sense of the presence of God.

From 1999 Etienne Maritz, the minister of three congregations of the Dutch Reformed Church, two in Namibia and one in Pretoria, South Africa, had been visiting the Netherlands where his ministry was especially blest among young people. During his years in the three congregations the Lord had blessed them with revival and he was invited to preach across South Africa on evangelism, prayer and revival. This became a full-time ministry from 1999 until he was called home to be with the Lord in December 2016.

HEART CRY CONFERENCES

From 2005 'Stichting Heart Cry' organized every year two big conferences with between 650 to 1250 visitors. In the autumn of 2005 Perold de Beer, a retired minister from South Africa, came to the Netherlands. At one of the conferences the Lord came down on the last Sunday evening and a score of young people were so convicted and broken that Perold spent the whole night giving pastoral care.

Chapter 9

In June 2006 Etienne Maritz was again in the Netherlands. He had seen revival in his own church in Koppies in South Africa and there was much expectancy. At the end of his visit, a conference was held in Ambt Delden with the theme 'Knowing God in a deeper way'. Over six hundred attended, mostly young people and young couples with their children. The days were described as 'like days of heaven on earth'.

Between the meetings, everywhere groups of young people were praying and singing and talking about the things of God. The last Sunday evening after the services, some four hundred stayed behind and a woman of around forty years who suffered for seventeen years with multiple problems gave her testimony how wonderfully the Lord had met her, and how her soul was set at liberty. The effect was wonderful. There came a moving of the Spirit and people began to weep and sob. The presence of God became so awesome and holy that nobody dared to talk, they could only whisper. Some were even trembling, shaking or fainting. Most of the people did not know what was happening and said: 'What does this mean?' Others could explain, 'This is that' (Acts 2:12,16).

Everywhere there were people praying, weeping, and confessing their sins, and it went on for hours. In the big meeting-room the people gathered who needed spiritual help, and it was about six am before Etienne and others finished counselling. There must have been at least one hundred people, and probably many more, who were powerfully touched and changed by the Lord. Many were awakened, convicted, and converted; backsliders were healed, lukewarm Christians made fervent, others set free from all kinds of problems, or led to assurance of faith or to renewed surrender to God. Bad marriages were restored, and good marriages made better. Most were so filled with the joy of God's salvation, that their tongues were loosened to talk of what God had done for their souls.

TESTIMONIES

Etienne Maritz made a visit to the Netherlands from 22 June to 4 July 2006, and wrote:

'It was my sixth visit to the Netherlands. The high-time was the big conference on the last weekend. More than six hundred people came, mostly working young people, unmarried, just married, or married with young children. The message dealt with the life in Christ and a deeper relation with God.

'On Saturday the Spirit of prayer came over the place and after the evening service big groups of young people prayed till the morning hours, while a few of us gave pastoral counselling. A woman, was delivered that evening from an evil spirit, and with tears of gladness started singing with the nearest prayer group: 'He has seen my need and delivered me...' The following evening the Lord was powerfully present in the preaching. Afterwards the same woman witnessed with power of her deliverance.

'Then I asked that when people wanted to accept the Lord or needed counselling, they would stay behind. Suddenly the Lord was in our midst and He took over. A young girl and an older lady fainted, in the presence of the Lord. Both came to conversion and were wonderfully set free. The young girl had been for years sexually molested by both her parents. Then we were overwhelmed by people in tears and brokenness, asking for prayer and counselling. About ten of us prayed right through the night with people. Others walked out of the meeting-room, softly and in holy respect for the presence of God. Without words they spontaneously formed prayer groups.

'I had the feeling that everything went beyond our control and God took over completely. Many people in South Africa and the Netherlands have prayed before and during the services and God answered their prayers. It was really as if we were living in the book of Acts. Every service was prayed through and full of power.'

Chapter 9

Abigail, a daughter of Hans and Aletta Pieterman, was at the conference and was eighteen at the time.

'At the beginning of the conference we were asked to pray specifically for what we expected to receive from the Lord during this weekend. I prayed that the Lord would remove everything what was hindering Him, in order that He might more and more be formed in me. For me personally it was a very blessed weekend, wherein all consciousness of time disappeared. Only a few hours of sleep was sufficient for us. I went to sleep with the presence of God and got up in His presence. I experienced His presence especially in the access to the mercy seat of God. When I prayed, it was as if I felt no separation anymore between God and me. No separation between heaven and earth. It was as if the presence of God was tangible. And the Lord allowed Himself to be prevailed on.

'On Sunday evening, time was given for testimonies. When a woman told the conference how God had delivered her from the devil, the influence of God's Spirit became overwhelming. The ground where we were became, as it were, holy ground. There was no talking, only whispering and weeping. When it was time to close the conference, we did not know how to. In silence we went outside, where the tables were full of drinks. But the cups remained untouched. Nobody had need of them. We went in great numbers to a tent where the presence of God was felt in such a way that there was much brokenness and humiliation. I was sitting in a group of ten to fifteen people. There was not one among us who did not come to the Lord in contrition and conviction of sin to ask forgiveness.

'Never will I forget how a man prayed with such an awe of God and with such a feeling of the holiness of God. He began his prayer with 'Holy, holy, holy is the Lord.' And it was so still … So still! And how he then drew near to God. We prayed until the middle of the night, supplicating and wrestling at God's mercy seat, for the salvation of lost souls, for the need of our native country, for a powerful work of the Lord, and much more. All this was the footsteps of His presence.'

Another who was there added:

'There came a call for prayer. With many we went to the big tent. What we experienced there is not to be described with a pen. The prayers to God were persevering, powerful, fervent and intense ... I have seen something of His glory. I wished that it should not stop. When someone started to sing a psalm, the sound was so heavenly—a little part of heaven on earth.'

Hans Pieterman concludes:

After that divine visitation on the conference of June/July 2006, many were wondering what would happen on the next 'Heart Cry' conference in September. As expected, there were even more visitors—about seven or eight hundred. The theme of the conference was 'That God is still living!' This time there were more prayer meetings, and some were attended by hundreds; also, until late into the night groups were praying and singing. Probably more people sought pastoral counselling than at the earlier conference, perhaps as many as a few hundred. A remarkable feature was, that many of them were seeking the Lord for forgiveness, so that even special meetings were arranged to speak about saving faith and assurance of salvation. When Mary Peckham had given her testimony of how the Lord met her in the days of the Lewis revival, she was afterwards surrounded by a number of weeping young girls searching for Christ.

The conferences still meet twice a year and the Lord continues to give His rich blessings, but there were no divine visitations like that in 2006.

10. From here to where?

There can be no doubt that revival is a phenomenon that has occurred regularly throughout the history of the Christian church and that true revival has always been for the benefit of the church, the community, and the honour of God. We have also shown that revival is an experience found both in the Old and New Testaments and that we may pray for it with a believing expectancy. If the church today assailed heaven through intelligent and persistent prayer for the right thing with the right motives, then we could expect to see God respond. This does not mean that we could anticipate inevitable revival, but God will not be deaf to the cry of his people.

Resistance to revival

Two opposite and equal dangers confront us. On the one hand, we may decide that revival is not for the church today because the day of grace has passed and things can only get worse—in consequence we do nothing. On the other hand, we may conclude that until God comes in revival there is no hope for the unbelief of the world or the lethargy and coldness of the church—in consequence we do nothing.

Every generation of Christians believes itself to be living in a godless age, and most consider that things have rarely been so bad; in this we are no different today from our forefathers before any revival. In fact, unless we are aware of the badness of our age, we are hardly likely to long for, or pray for, revival. Society's values today—politically, economically, morally and spiritually—are in collision with God's law. But so they were in the Middle Ages before Wycliffe, and in the eighteenth century before Whitefield, and in the nineteenth century before Spurgeon. Our plea with

God for revival must only be based upon the dishonour that the present weakness of the church brings upon him.

Some may not want revival because in their church it is unthinkable that any 'glorious disorder' should take over from the set agenda that has been followed for years with faithful monotony. Revival is a time of unpredictable things, and for some, it is the uncertainty that worries them. All our churches and fellowships, whatever our label, have a programme: our meetings are planned, activities arranged, and speakers are booked for some way ahead. There is nothing wrong with all that. But revival makes changes. And some of us don't like change. On the other hand, there are Christians who live and worship with inglorious disorder all the time, and God may send them a revival of glorious order.

When Count Zinzendorf explained that, before the revival of 1727 in Moravia, 'We had been the leaders and helpers,' but that afterwards, 'The Holy Spirit himself took full control of everything and everybody', he was not criticizing the way the leaders had gone about their work before revival. They had been faithful 'shepherds, serving as overseers' (1 Peter 5:2), and they would be so again; but when revival came the leaders were aware of standing aside and watching God at work. God's Spirit will never work contrary to his own revealed word, but there is such a rich diversity of his working revealed in Scripture that this gives him much room to manoeuvre. It is God's sudden, unpredictable and overpowering work that is a threat to some Christians.

> It is God's sudden, unpredictable and overpowering work that is a threat to some Christians

Others are doubtful because of the changed times. We see the circumstances as very different today. Wycliffe at least brought the Bible to a religious people who needed no persuading that God was real; they only needed the Scriptures to show them the truth about God and salvation. Wesley and Whitefield preached in a day when the public sermon was still expected, and in the open air it was a novelty. Three godless young men were converted at Cambuslang in 1742 simply because after breakfast they decided to go and 'hear a sermon' before they continued their journey to enjoy themselves with the pleasures that Edinburgh had to offer. Today, we can hardly imagine three men on their way to the races spending time listening to a sermon.

During the 1860s when William Haslam was preaching in Lowestoft a man went from boat to boat to gather a congregation of fishermen to hear him. By 1921 in the same fishing port it was not so easy, but even then many fishermen attended London Road Baptist Church during the herring season. When Haslam preached in Scotland in the 1860s an Englishman preaching was a sufficient novelty to attract a crowd. Duncan Campbell admitted that when he preached in the Western Islands of Scotland in the 1940s and 50s he preached to a people with a Bible tradition and a history of revivals.

Until the second half of the twentieth century, it appeared that men only needed a loud voice to awaken them out of their sleep of death, but today that sleep is a drugged unconsciousness. Minds are captured by a false philosophy and world view, false religion and the comforts of this world. Every generation sees the nation slipping further away from the truth and more set in its opposition to God. It is hard to imagine revival in many Western churches in the twenty-first century.

But all this is human reasoning. Our concern whether today's generation may be beyond the reach even of revival assumes that there is a limit to God's power—that there is a hardness of heart and confusion of mind into which even God cannot break. No Christian can allow themselves to be sucked into this kind of thinking. Certainly, the days are hard and the minds of most are spiritually drugged; certainly, life is different today from that in any previous century. But there is one constant for the evangelical Christian, and that constant is God. When we abandon him we abandon hope. We dare not doubt God. If the days are harder, then all the more glory will belong to God when he brings revival.

Some Christians are fearful of revival for another reason—and they may have good cause to be. Revival is a time of deep searching by the Holy Spirit when sins of mind and habit are found out by God. In revival we do not ask God to reveal our sin to us—he does. In revival Christians who are reading books and magazines, or watching programmes or films, that are slowly strangling their spiritual life will be forced to confess these things before God, if not before the church. The Christian cherishing a secret 'affair' or habit, or harbouring the gain of dishonest dealing, will be forced into the open. Bitterness, hatred and resentment will have to be dealt with. Revival is the work of the Holy Spirit; and holiness and revival are inseparable. When Evan Roberts prayed, 'Bend the Church and save the world,' this is what he meant. Only the Christian who is striving to be holy and whose conscience is touch-sensitive to sin need not fear revival.

Others may be fearful because revival is often followed by a time of testing or persecution. This is an understandable fear of those living in times when revival seems so distant and even unreal. However, when revival comes there is such new life and certain confidence in God that Christians simply do not fear the future. Besides, the joy and privilege of revival far outweigh any suffering that may follow. For Christians who fear revival for this reason, their only refuge should be in the fact that God's will for his people is always 'good, pleasing and perfect' (Romans 12:2). We need never be afraid when God is in control.

Longing for revival

A young Christian approached me after a series that had surveyed the accounts of revivals in a biblical context: 'It's all very depressing', she suggested, 'because things just aren't like this today.' I understood her problem. Many Christians find the story of revival frankly discouraging. A time of revival is so different from the days of hard work for small returns; and the more we look at revival, the smaller our successes appear in comparison. You can work for a long time in the gathering darkness until you look up at a distant light, then suddenly everything around you is black. Revival is a distant light that may distract our attention just long enough to spoil our vision for working into the night. But surely it is no bad thing to be reminded how much better we could work with a light on.

The study of God's mighty works in the past is never meant to discourage us. We may find it disconcerting, but we should not be discouraged, least of all depressed. The church has a task to do now, and daydreaming about how God might intervene does not get it done. The story of revival should be an incentive to harder work, more earnest prayer and holier living. More rewards of 'Well done, good and faithful servant,' are earned in the normal days of the church's constant battle against sin and the devil than in the heady delights of revival. It is not hard to preach the gospel and witness to the neighbour when Christ is the topic of the community's conversation; but there is a particular courage needed when few are responding and the gospel is despised. To those who are discouraged, the story of revivals should prove a great incentive and encouragement to go on in hope: 'Like cold water to a weary soul is good news from a distant land' (Proverbs 25:25).

> 'Like cold water to a weary soul is good news from a distant land'

Many Christians pray occasionally for revival; others will listen enthusiastically and talk excitedly of the great acts of God in revival; a few will set themselves to plead with God, whatever the cost and however long it takes. That is what is needed today.

The events of revival are what God expects to be present in the life of his church normally; but a revival is when these things are heightened and intensified to such a degree that they become something unusual and can only be described as supernormal. Or, to put it another way, God does not expect his church to be in continuous revival, but revival reveals those ingredients God expects always to be present. This is why it is a good thing to read and study what God's word tells us about revival and also what

God has done in revivals in the story of the church. In this way we begin to see something of what God expects us to be now. Whatever we find in a true revival we should be striving for now. By doing this we show God that we are serious about the business of wanting revival. There is no revival for those who do nothing and want nothing.

The significant thing for us about the letters in Revelation is that God did not promise to revive them out of their disobedience or backsliding. On the contrary, he says to Ephesus, 'repent' (2:5), to Smyrna, 'be faithful' (2:10), to Pergamum, 'repent' (2:16), to Thyatira, 'hold on' (3:11) and to Laodicea, 'be earnest and repent' (3:19). Each time God places the answer in the hands of his people, whilst at the same time recognizing their helplessness without him. Always God places the responsibility upon us; God never encourages us to wait in lazy inactivity for him to take the initiative, even though it is in fact God who takes the initiative.

> God never encourages us to wait in lazy inactivity for him to take the initiative

Therefore, we must go on doing those things that we know will please God; this is the way we prepare ourselves. We must work and witness now, however hard the way. We must sow in tears and in hope, and confidently expect that we shall 'reap with songs of joy' (Psalm 126:5). And if we go on preparing ourselves, here and there we shall at least enjoy the outskirts of revival.

God expects his people to be doing constantly those things which he will take up in revival and use in a quite unexpected way; but we must never imagine that we can create a revival simply by imitating those elements that accompany it. And we dare not try to achieve by our plans and programmes what God alone, by his Holy Spirit, can do. Revival is God's sovereign work. It is his to give, but ours to long for, prepare for, pray for and perhaps to receive. He may wait, but we must work and worry God so that when he comes we are ready and he will not pass us by.

David Morgan, who was greatly used by God during the 1859 revival in Wales, felt he could see the approach of an outpouring of the Spirit and wrote in his diary during 1855: 'By reading the history of the Church we find that the great cause fluctuates up and down through the ages, but that, whenever the Lord drew near to save there was some considerable expectancy amongst the godly for His coming. As well as praying, we should be doing our utmost to revive the work. So did the godly of old: they prayed and they worked.'[67]

A year before the revival of 1859, a minister in Aberdare put forward suggestions for preparing for revival. These included 'a pure ministry … apostolic preaching … the awakening must start in the pulpit … the church must be in full sympathy with the ministry … the particular use of the means of grace … earnest prayer'.[68]

In 1907 Dr A. C. Dixon was preaching at Charlotte Chapel in Edinburgh. The church was enjoying a time of revival under the leadership of its minister, Joseph Kemp, and had recently rebuilt to accommodate the rapidly increasing attendance. Dr Dixon warned the church of the danger of losing all that God had for them. His warning is just as relevant for those who are praying for revival. Nothing will hinder the corning of the Spirit more easily than slack, undisciplined and ungodly living. Dr Dixon reminded his congregation:

'Every Revival movement is a call for watchfulness, the present being no exception. If this work of grace is to be conserved, every member of the church must guard well his and her own behaviour. Do nothing that will grieve the Spirit of God. He is so sensitive, and may pass from us without our having received the full blessing he desires to give us. Let all evil be put away from us. Let our home life be consistent with our profession. Let us be on our guard in conversation. Utter no word of

---

67 Evans, *When He is Come* (SMW, 1959), p. 25.
68 As above, p. 31.

disparagement concerning any brother. Speak to God oftener about one another's faults, and there will be fewer faults to speak about. Do not neglect family and private prayer. Be in attendance at the church prayer meetings. Instantly obey the Spirit's promptings, and if he suggests to you to speak to souls about eternal matters, do it without questioning. He will give the grace and power.' [69]

Praying for revival

If we believe in the necessity and the possibility of revival, most Christians will acknowledge the importance of prayer. But acknowledgement and action are often a world apart. A passing request for revival, even repeated daily, is hardly the same as a heart-cry for God to take action in defence of his name and his honour. There are few prayer meetings today that are wholly committed to revival, and even fewer that take seriously the need to present a reasoned and responsive case before God.

There is probably no such thing as a typical prayer meeting, but to commence with a corporate act of worship focusing upon the Triune God (and not our own experiences) can never be misplaced. A brief introduction to an historical revival (or aspect of revival) establishes and clarifies what we are longing for and reminds everyone of the historical reality of our subject. The cameos of eyewitnesses to revival given in the previous chapter will certainly focus a prayer meeting on real revival. But it is essential that a passage of Scripture should be read and explained, in a way similar to the examples given in chapter eight. In this way we may be driven to prayer not simply by the desperate state of our society or our church, but by the encouragement of Scripture.

> God will respond to his people when their hearts are right, their minds informed, their lives consistent and their cause is good

---

69 Kemp, *Joseph W. Kemp* (Marshall, Morgan & Scott, 1936), p.61.

God will respond to his people when their hearts are right, their minds informed, their lives consistent and their cause is good. There is no better way to ensure all of these than by placing ourselves under the instruction and incentive of Scripture. A disobedient people can never expect to be heard by God: '"When I called, they did not listen; so when they called, I would not listen," says the LORD Almighty' (Zechariah 7:13. Also Proverbs 1:25,26).

This can be hard work. It means we can no longer idly toss Bible passages towards heaven on the assumption that our intention is what matters. God expects his people to handle his word with care, and that means with thought. Perhaps, after all, it is not just our sin that stands in the way of God pouring out his Spirit in revival, but our ignorance of that tool which he has placed into our hands to persuade him.

Jonathan Edwards and a union of prayer for revival

In 1744 a group of four ministers in Scotland agreed that for two years they would set aside time every Saturday evening and Sunday morning and the first Tuesday of each quarter, either part or whole of the day (as duties allowed) in prayer for revival. This could be in private groups, public meetings or alone in secret. In this way, Christians would be encouraged to know that many in distant places would be praying at the same time. Nothing would be advertised in the press, but this 'union of prayer' would be spread through personal conversation. The invitation was 'not restricted to any denomination or party' but to those 'who have at heart the interest of vital Christianity, and the power of godliness; and who, however differing about other things, are convinced of the importance of fervent prayer, to promote that common interest, and of Scripture-persuasives to promote such prayer.'

This 'concert of prayer' had begun in 1743 in Kilsyth under the leadership of James Robe, the minister of that town, and by the end of the year there were thirty groups of young people, some with more than thirty members, and even more groups in Glasgow.

In November 1745 the ministers sent out a letter urging the continuation of these prayer meetings for a further seven years. Five hundred copies of the letter arrived in New England and this 'concert of prayer' so captured the mind of Jonathan Edwards that he expounded at length on the whole concept. It ran to almost 58,000 words and was published in Boston, New England in 1747 under the title:

AN HUMBLE ATTEMPT to promote an explicit Agreement and visible Union of God's People thro' the World, in extraordinary PRAYER, for the REVIVAL of Religion and the Advancement of Christ's Kingdom on Earth, pursuant to Scripture-Promises and Prophecies concerning the last Time.

Edwards' appeal was based on Zechariah 8:20–22 (Authorised Version):

'Thus saith the LORD of hosts; *It shall yet come to pass,*
     that there shall come people,
And the inhabitants of many cities:
And the inhabitants of one city shall go to another, saying,
Let us go speedily to pray before the LORD,
And to seek the LORD of hosts: I will go also.
Yea, many people and strong nations shall come
To seek the LORD of hosts in Jerusalem,
And to pray before the LORD.'

Edwards was convinced that 'the Jewish nation were to have a share, and a very eminent and distinguishing share', in the fulfilment of this prophecy, and that the 'whole chapter, beyond all dispute, has respect to the most glorious state of the Church of God on earth.' He added that up until now, 'There has been nothing yet brought to pass, in any measure to answer these prophecies.' It was a commitment to Edwards' postmillennial hope which was shared by most of his contemporaries on both sides of the Atlantic.

Edwards referred to the duty of prayer, the good that is the object of prayer, those who prayed in such unity, the mode of their union, the manner in which they prayed, and the context of the prayer.

The greater part of his *Humble Attempt* was a detailed nine-point exposition of his total conviction that, 'It is evident from the Scripture, that there is yet remaining a great advancement of the interest of religion and the kingdom of Christ in this world, by an abundant outpouring of the Spirit of God, far greater and more extensive than ever yet has been.'

After responding to various objections that could be raised to such a union of prayer, Edwards concluded:

'The Ministers that make this proposal to us, are quiet and peaceable members and ministers of the Church of Scotland, that have lamented the late divisions and breaches of that Church. For my part, I sincerely wish and hope, that there may not be an end of extraordinary united prayer, among God's people, for the effusions of the blessed Spirit, when the seven years are ended, but that it will be continued.'

The effect of this Concert of Prayer for revival was widespread. To give only one example:[70] As late as 1784 The Baptist pastor, John Ryland, introduced the *Humble Attempt* to his colleagues Andrew Fuller and John Sutcliffe. They were so challenged by it that they recommended a similar union for prayer to the Calvinistic Baptist churches and beyond. Many see this as the main event leading to the Second Evangelical Awakening from 1790 to 1830.[71]

---

70 An excellent article available on line: 'John Sutcliffe and the Concert of Prayer' by Michael Haykin, *Reformation and Revival*, Summer 1992.

71 J. Edwin Orr, *The Eager Feet: Evangelical Awakenings, 1790-1830*, pp. 95, 191–92, 199 (Moody Press, Chicago 1975).

If we have come this far in general agreement in our study of a biblical basis for revival, then we should have gained a determination to seek God through intelligent and persistent prayer. Such a response can only be healthy for his people. If the church today assailed heaven for the right thing, to the right end and with the right reasons, then we could expect to see God respond. We cannot anticipate inevitable revival, but such diligent searching for God will always be heard, because God is a very good listener.

Is revival the only hope for the church of Christ? Of course not! Across the world there are serious and faithful congregations with a deep love for Christ, worshipping and working together in harmony and love; there are Christian leaders of faultless character leading their people in spiritual wisdom, and there are gospel preachers who, loyally and without fear, proclaim nothing but the truth of God's word. This, together with the guarantee of our Saviour, is the hope for the future growth of the church. Our understanding of the Scriptures should lead us to the conclusion that however glorious revival is and however much it increases the numerical and spiritual vigour of the church, it is not essential to the growth and existence of the church worldwide.

Perhaps revival is not even the church's finest hour. During the second and third centuries of the church, thousands of Christians, both men and women, were brutally tortured and gruesomely martyred for their refusal to deny the Saviour who had died for them, and they were not all living in times of revival. Those where some of the finest days of the history of the church. Ever since then to the present day there has been a stream of martyrs for Christ. It is reliably calculated that there are more martyrs for Jesus each year in our time than in the entire previous history of the Christian church. The church in the fires of persecution is so often the church at her finest.

The church in the fires of persecution is so often the church at her finest

This may be an unexpected ending to such a study as this, but however much we may long for and believe in revival, those who are first in the Kingdom of God are not necessarily those who lived during times of spiritual revival, but those who persevered when all around seemed to give way. Soldiers prove themselves on the rugged terrain in the face of a vigorous and vicious enemy, not on the quiet beaches of a tropical paradise. More honours are won by those who maintain their morale and courage when the tide of battle is running against them than in the heady days of victory.

To repeat what we said in the introduction to this book, we must learn to be a people satisfied with God even when we are not yet saturated with God. A satisfied dissatisfaction is one of those necessary paradoxes of the Christian life. Besides, revival should never be the *all-consuming* concern of the church. Good things can happen for the church and through the church even on the outside of revival.

We can only end where *Revival—a people saturated with God* also concludes:

Nothing must be allowed to hinder our work in the 'ordinary times'. Our life of prayer, our striving for holiness, and our wholehearted evangelism must all go on as if the future of the church of Christ depended upon them. However, at the same time we must long for our community to be 'saturated with God', we ought often to be talking of the great acts of God in revival, and our prayers should continually remind God that we need a 'special occasion' for this generation.

The prophet Micah could find little to encourage him in the nation. An honest assessment convinced him that the forces of evil were gaining ground. However, Micah set out his own position:

> **'As for me, I watch in hope for the LORD,**
> **I wait for God my Saviour; my God will hear me'**
> (Micah 7:7).

Scripture index

Scripture index

Scripture index

Revival
A people saturated with God

Brian H Edwards

288pp | ISBN 978-1-84625-647-9
REF REVPSG6431 | £9.00

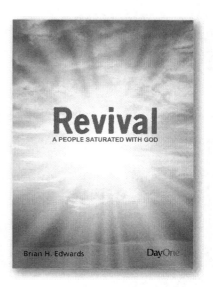

This book is the twin of the current volume. It answers the question: What is 'revival' in the history of the Christian church and how can we distinguish a genuine work of God's Spirit from the false claims that often distract us? The hallmarks of God's special occasions across the centuries and across the continents are gathered together to present a thrilling account of God's great work in spiritual revival.

'This treasure trove well-deserves a place in every Christian home. Following the Old Testament example of praying for a spiritual awakening by hearing what God did in the past, the narratives and testimonies of revival unmask our spiritual poverty and fuel a desire for God to awaken us today to pray that he will "in wrath remember mercy".'

—SINCLAIR FERGUSON, *Chancellor's Professor of Systematic Theology at the Reformed Theological Seminary and Teaching Fellow, Ligonier Ministries.*

'In researching the history of revivals we hear another language almost unknown in the modern church with its emphasis on methodology and management. I defy you to read this excellent book and not long with fresh urgency for God to come with revival and to do in our generation what he has repeatedly done in the past.'

—TERRY VIRGO, *Preacher, writer and founder of Newfrontiers.*

'Here is a thrilling account of God's special work in revival over many centuries. It is a wise guide to interpreting these events, helpfully bringing together the common factors and sovereignty of God and critiquing some of the excesses that may accompany revival. I encourage everyone to read this book. It will stir our hearts to long for more of the felt presence of God.'

—JOHN STEVENS, *National Director, The Fellowship of Independent Evangelical Churches.*

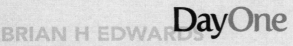
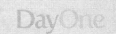

ALL YOU NEED TO KNOW ABOUT THE BIBLE

'...A wealth of material in readable style, it is a rich resource, giving fresh confidence in the reliability and authority of the Scriptures.'
—BILL JAMES, Principal, The London Seminary

'...Brian has the skill to make this subject accessible without simplification or omission... What a great resource for Christians.'
—ADRIAN REYNOLDS, FIEC Training Director

'...Accessible throughout, Brian writes in a manner that will benefit the newest Christian. I hope his work receives the widest possible readership.'
—DR ROBERT LETHAM, Union School of Theology, Wales

'...A feast of wisdom and insight into the origins and accuracy of the Bible...These volumes will be of assistance to every Bible student.'
—DR ANDREW ATHERSTONE, Latimer Research Fellow, Wycliffe Hall, Oxford

'...A superb collection, readable and reliable... A terrific resource for both believers and those seeking faith. Highly recommended!'
—DR STEVE BRADY, Principal, Moorlands College, Christchurch

'...These books serve well to helpfully answer numerous objections, confirm faith, and wisely guide in profitable reading of the Word.'
—DR JOEL R. BEEKE, Puritan Reformed Theological Seminary, Michigan

DayOne

EVIDENCE for the BIBLE

Clive Anderson and
Brian Edwards

LARGE FORMAT HARDBACK
FULL COLOUR THROUGHOUT
225mm × 275mm
260pp | ISBN 978-1-84625-416-1
REF EFB4161 | £25.00

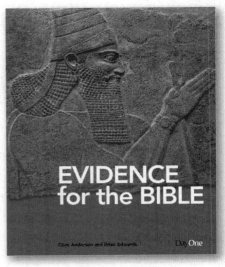

Evidence will surprise and inform you as you turn over the soil of history with the pages of your Bible. The witness of the trowel authenticates and illuminates the people and events, lifting them from the pages of the Book and setting them in the context of time and place. Join us on an exciting journey with this evidence from the past.

Evidence for the Bible can be found in many places, from the Ancient Near East to museums and private collections. Whilst artefacts can never prove the authority of the Bible, they can and do show that the events described in the Bible occurred in time and history.

This book provides a selection of the many items that demonstrate the reliability of the Bible as a historical document.

'Clive Anderson and Brian Edwards have captured the essence of generations of middle-eastern archaeology, historical context and biblical landscape in a quite remarkable way. Their book is accessible, informative and enjoyable. The pictures beautifully complement the text. The Bible comes alive. I warmly and wholeheartedly commend it to everyone who wishes to be a little wiser and better informed about the Book which has formed our culture and is the source of the Christian Faith.'

THE VERY REVD JAMES ATWELL,
Dean of Winchester.

'This is a marvellous introduction to the finds of archaeology that illumine our understanding of the Bible. It helps the reader to see that the biblical events and writings took place within history. When the reader studies the Bible, this book will serve as a wonderful tool to help get at its depth and richness. I highly recommend it.'

DR JOHN D CURRID
Carl McMurray Professor of Old Testament at the Reformed Theological Seminary, Charlotte, USA.

Grace— amazing grace

Brian H Edwards

304pp | ISBN 978-1-84625-336-2
REF GRACE | £9.00

'Grace is the most beautiful word in our language and the supreme description of God.' With these opening words the author introduces his theme, and in seventeen chapters portrays the grace of God in its vast array. In a popular and penetrating style, the author compels us forward with theology for the heart. This book is firmly theological, warmly devotional and incisively practical.

Brian Edwards questions the commonly accepted positions in 'forgiving grace', provides a robust chapter on 'universal grace' and a moving chapter on 'incarnate grace'. In particular his approach to 'ultimate grace' is an intriguing and fitting conclusion to the whole subject. The questions at the close of each chapter make this an excellent book for small group discussion.

'As Brian Edwards tells us, "Grace encompasses all the great truths of Christianity, for without grace they would have no meaning." He then guides us on a delightful tour that takes us from God's common grace for all mankind to the ultimate grace of heaven for God's people. I have never read anything better on the subject than this superb and sure-footed treatment.'

DR JOHN BLANCHARD, *evangelist, author and Christian apologist*

The Ten Commandments

for today

Brian H Edwards

288pp | ISBN 978-1-90308-733-6
REF 10T | £9.00

At a time when the nation's morality is in alarming decline, it is surprising that so little has been written on the Ten Commandments. This modern commentary carefully uncovers their true meaning and incisively applies them to our contemporary society. Probably never in the history of western civilisation have the Ten Commandments been more neglected and therefore more relevant than today.

This book is a superbly written modern commentary on God's changeless laws in today's changing and godless society.

'This book unpacks the crammed meaning of these terse commands, and applies them pointedly to life in a deregulated age.'
ANDREW ANDERSON

'This is a highly readable treatment of a vital subject and can be gratefully recommended."
EVANGELICAL TIMES

'Seldom have I appreciated a book more than this one…'
THE GOSPEL MAGAZINE